In Search of
Schopenhauer's Cat

In Search of Schopenhauer's Cat

Arthur Schopenhauer's
Quantum-Mystical Theory
of Justice

Raymond B. Marcin

The Catholic University of America Press
Washington, D.C.

Copyright © 2006

The Catholic University of America Press

All rights reserved

The paper used in this publication meets the minimum requirements of American National Standards for Information Science—Permanence of Paper for Printed Library Materials, ANSI Z39.48-1984.

∞

Library of Congress Cataloging-in-Publication Data

Marcin, Raymond B., 1938–

In search of Schopenhauer's cat : Arthur Schopenhauer's quantum-mystical theory of justice / Raymond B. Marcin.—1st ed.

    p. cm.

    Includes bibliographical references and index.

    ISBN-13: 978-0-8132-1430-6 (hardcover : alk. paper)

    ISBN-13: 978-0-8132-2831-0 (pbk.)

    1. Schopenhauer, Arthur, 1788–1860. 2. Justice (Philosophy). I. Title.

B3148.M34 2006

193—dc22

2005011526

For Judy

[I]n all that happens or indeed can happen to the individual, justice is always done to it.

—*Arthur Schopenhauer*

Contents

Acknowledgments ix

Introduction xi

1. Schopenhauer's Life   1
2. Kant's Influence   11
3. Schopenhauer's Departure from Kant   18
4. Schopenhauer's Own Claim to Fame   27
5. Platonic Ideas   33
6. Schopenhauer and Contemporary Scientific Theory   38
7. Ontological "Oneness"   44
8. Justice and the *Principium Individuationis*   62
9. The Inner Conflict   68
10. A Brief Glimpse into Theistic Natural Law Theory   74
11. Eternal Justice   93
12. The Denial of the Will to Live   104
13. Schopenhauer and Quietism   116
14. Schopenhauer and Luther   134
15. On the Freedom of the Will   140
16. Modern Conceptions of Justice   147
17. Schopenhauer and Contemporary Political Thought   174

Bibliography   181

Index   189

Acknowledgments

I wish to express my gratitude to David E. Cartwright, Ph.D., and Steven Neeley, J.D., Ph.D., for their excellent and constructive critiques and recommendations on the manuscript for this book; to Attorney Jack Himmelstein for introducing me to the quantum philosophy of David Bohm, and to Professors George P. Smith, Marshall Breger, and Douglas Kmiec for many years of friendship and encouragement.

Introduction

The philosophy of Arthur Schopenhauer has surprising affinities with many of the current teachings of quantum physics and also with many of the historic tenets of Eastern philosophy and Western religious mysticism. In the course of its romp through that quantum-mystical worldview, it presents a startlingly unique conception of justice. Schopenhauer's philosophy really does not have very much at all to do with cats, but, in 1844, writing in the second volume of his magnum opus, *The World as Will and Representation*, Arthur Schopenhauer made one curious statement about a cat (or cats). He wrote:

> I know quite well that anyone would regard me as mad if I seriously assured him that the cat, playing just now in the yard, is still the same one that did the same jumps and tricks three hundred years ago; but I also know that it is much more absurd to believe that the cat of today is through and through and fundamentally an entirely different one from the cat of three hundred years ago.[1]

[1]. Arthur Schopenhauer, *The World as Will and Representation*, vol. 2 (1844), trans. E. F. J. Payne (New York: Dover Books, 1969), 482 (hereinafter, *WWR*-2).

Amazingly enough, Schopenhauer defended that statement throughout both volumes of his masterwork and indeed throughout all his other philosophical writings. As we shall see below if we accept the main tenet of his philosophy, that is, that the world is both "will" and "re-presentation," the cat indeed both *is* and *is not* the same cat that frolicked in Schopenhauer's yard three hundred years ago.

Almost one hundred years later, in 1935, quantum physicist Erwin Schrödinger, who had a profound knowledge of the writings of Schopenhauer,[2] and whose scientific work similarly did not have very much at all to do with cats, suggested a "thought experiment," also involving a *cat*. Whether his knowledge of Schopenhauer's writings was responsible for his selection of a cat to illustrate his point is problematic. Schrödinger created a scenario in which a hypothetical cat in a hypothetical box would have to be both dead and alive at the same time, if certain widely held tenets of quantum theory are correct.[3] By the 1980s, the cat-in-the-box thought experiment had become so central to the development of quantum physics that Cambridge astrophysicist John Gribben featured it in the very title of his popular presentation of the history of quantum theory, *In Search of Schrödinger's Cat: Quantum Physics and Reality*, probably the best and most widely read popular introduction to quantum physics. In the 1990s, with Schrödinger's cat-in-the-box paradox still besetting the world of the quantum physicists, Gribben published a sequel, *Schrödinger's Kittens and the Search for Reality: Solving the Quantum Mysteries*,[4] in which he posed his own thought experiment involving

---

2. Erwin Schrödinger, *My View of the World* (originally published by Paul Zsolnay Verlag GMBH, 1961), trans. Cecily Hastings (Woodbridge, Conn.: Ox Bow Press, 1983), viii (hereinafter, Schrödinger).

3. See John Gribben, *In Search of Schrödinger's Cat: Quantum Physics and Reality* (New York: Bantam Books, 1984), 2–3, 203–8 (hereinafter, Gribben, *Cat*).

4. John Gribben, *Schrödinger's Kittens and the Search for Reality: Solving the Quantum Mysteries* (Boston: Little, Brown, 1995) (hereinafter, Gribben, *Kittens*).

two descendants of Schrödinger's cat, each necessarily both alive and dead at the same time.

I explain both thought experiments, Schrödinger's and Gribben's, in further detail in the book. If Erwin Schrödinger did not get his "cat" idea from reading Schopenhauer, then it is one of those serendipitous coincidences of science and philosophy that, with almost a century separating them, Schrödinger and Schopenhauer both happened to involve a cat (or cats) in their efforts to communicate understandings of reality and philosophies of being that are actually quite similar. Moreover, as we shall see, the fact that Schopenhauer's cats were widely separated by *time* itself may not prove to be irrelevant to the comparison of the thought-models, but again we must leave an exploration of the relevance for a later chapter of this book.

Those who are not well acquainted with the understandings of subatomic reality that have been emerging from quantum physics over the past century are invariably astonished whenever they begin to pursue that acquaintance. There is something strange, perhaps stranger than we can imagine, about reality at the deep down, subatomic, quantum, "micro" level. It is a realm in which the distinction between subject and object disappears, and all is a chaos of flux and probability. And yet, as bizarre and unimaginable as it may seem, something quite similar to that very understanding of reality was imagined and anticipated in the philosophy of Arthur Schopenhauer many decades before the beginnings of the development of quantum theory.

As to the "mystical" character of Schopenhauer's theory of justice, the connections between Schopenhauer's philosophy and religious mysticism have been acknowledged not only by quantum physicist Erwin Schrödinger,[5] but also by no less a personage than Albert Einstein:

5. Schrödinger, 96, 104.

> The individual [wrote Einstein] feels the futility of human desires and aims and the sublimity and marvelous order which reveal themselves both in nature and in the world of thought. Individual existence impresses him as a sort of prison and he wants to *experience the universe as a single significant whole.* The beginnings of cosmic religious feeling already appear at an early stage of development, for example, in many of the Psalms of David and in some of the Prophets. Buddhism, as we have learned *especially from the wonderful writings of Schopenhauer,* contains a much stronger element of this.[6]

It is appropriate that Albert Einstein referred to the writings of Schopenhauer as "wonderful," that is, full of wonder. Schopenhauer, following Kant, actually anticipated (from the vantage point of philosophy rather than of science, of course, and without the mathematics) Einstein's famed principle of the equivalence of matter and energy (presented by Einstein in the equation $e = mc^2$). Although the connection he drew between Schopenhauer's philosophy and Einstein's theory of matter/energy equivalence is tenuous, prolific Schopenhauer scholar Bryan Magee claimed to notice it:

> Perhaps the most astonishing of all the many Kantian-Schopenhauerian anticipations of modern science lies . . . in the former's very specific announcement of one of the central doctrines of Einstein's theory of relativity more than a century before Einstein—the doctrine that (as Schopenhauer put it, following Kant): "force and substance are inseparable because at bottom they are one."[7]

---

6. Albert Einstein, *Ideas and Opinions* (New York: Crown Publishers, 1954), quoted in Ken Wilber, ed., *Quantum Questions: Mystical Writings of the World's Greatest Physicists* (Boston: Shambhala, 2001), 104 (emphasis added).

7. Bryan Magee, *The Philosophy of Schopenhauer*, rev. ed. (Oxford: Clarendon Press, 1997), 112 (hereinafter, Magee). See also *WWR*-2, 309.

There is a curiosity about Schopenhauer. Most people know his name but little or nothing about his philosophy. The truth is that we would all be much better off if we knew something about his philosophy, but forgot his name, for Arthur Schopenhauer was a strange rarity—a prophet indeed, but a prophet who not only did not practice what he preached, but who made no pretensions of any sort of a moral duty to do so.

Schopenhauer's theory of justice, the reader should be cautioned, is radical in the extreme. Justice, in Schopenhauer's system, is not an epistemological construct. It is neither rights based nor process based. It rejects the concept of individual duty as vehemently as it embraces the concept of collective guilt. For Schopenhauer, justice is not a way of assessing reality; justice is a facet of reality itself. Schopenhauer's theory of justice is, thus, ontology—a study of being.

There are reasons why a review and a reevaluation of Schopenhauer's theory of justice are worthwhile now, almost two hundred years after it was first formulated. One is that his theory of justice, based squarely on his philosophy of being (or ontology), seems remarkably consistent with the view of reality that is taking shape in the minds of contemporary quantum physicists.[8] Another reason is that the metaphysical basis of Schopenhauer's theory of justice bridges a gap that has long existed between Western and Eastern approaches to philosophy.[9] Yet another reason is that some contempo-

---

8. For some other views of the relevance of contemporary quantum physics to modern understandings of law and justice, see, e.g., R. George Wright, "Should the Law Reflect the World?: Lessons for Legal Theory from Quantum Mechanics," *Florida State University Law Review* 18 (1991): 855; Michael J. Van Sistine and Bruce Meredith, "The Legality of Early Retirement Incentive Plans: Can Quantum Physics Help Resolve the Current Uncertainty," *Marquette Law Review* 84 (2001): 587; Avner Levin, "Quantum Physics in Private Law," *Canadian Journal of Law & Jurisprudence* 14 (2001): 249 ; Laurence Tribe, "The Curvature of Constitutional Space: What Lawyers Can Learn from Modern Physics," *Harvard Law Review* 103 (1989): 1; and Raymond B. Marcin, "Schopenhauer's Theory of Justice," *Catholic University Law Review* 43 (1994): 813.

9. See, e.g., Raymond B. Marcin, "Justice and Love," *Catholic University Law*

rary jurisprudential movements with a strong social orientation, for example, critical legal studies, civic republicanism, and so-called new legal process jurisprudence, have of late taken an interest in the concept of "community,"[10] and the idea of "comm-unity" in its most basic and most literal sense is at the heart of Schopenhauer's ontology of justice. Also, aspects of Schopenhauer's theory of justice—the aspects of justice that inhabit the everyday world of everyday phenomena—yield concepts of law and legal responsibility that are distinctly behaviorist in tone, and recent scholarship in the area of legal pragmatism and law-and-economics theory suggests a trend in the direction of behaviorism.[11] Finally, the concept of justice has almost always been examined, in the legal literature of the past and present, from an epistemological vantage point.[12] Seldom have we seen, outside the natural law tradition (a chapter on the natural law tradition and its relationship with Schopenhauerian justice is included below), a metaphysical or ontological examination of justice, and that is exactly what Schopenhauer gives us.

We first delve briefly into Schopenhauer's life story. Then we examine Schopenhauer's place in the line of Western philosophers, particularly his positioning with respect to Kant and Hegel. Then we follow with inquiries into Schopenhauer's metaphysics, the metaphysical bases of his theory of justice, the theory of justice proper,

---

Review 33 (1984): 363 (tracing the concept of justice from positivist and Rawlsian Western models to the Gandhian concepts of *ahimsa* and *Satyagraha*).

10. See, e.g., Mary Ann Glendon, *Rights Talk: The Impoverishment of Political Discourse* (New York: Free Press, 1991); Cass R. Sunstein, *After the Rights Revolution: Reconceiving the Regulatory State* (Cambridge: Harvard University Press, 1990); Stephen A. Gardbaum, "Law, Politics, and the Claims of Community," *Michigan Law Review* 90 (1992): 685; Symposium, "The Republican Civic Tradition," *Yale Law Journal* 97 (1988): 1493.

11. See, e.g., Richard A. Posner, *The Problems of Jurisprudence* (Cambridge: Harvard University Press, 1990), 169–84 (hereinafter, Posner).

12. One looks almost in vain through Western legal literature for a nondivisive, unifying understanding of the concept of justice that transcends the ideological pluralism which plagues us as a human society. See Raymond B. Marcin, "Justice and Love," *Catholic University Law Review* 33 (1984): 363, for just such a quest.

and some of its implications for the human condition. Interspersed throughout are analyses of the relationships between Schopenhauer's thought and contemporary quantum physics, Eastern philosophical approaches and understandings, Christian cultural and scriptural scholarship, and a form of predominantly Christian mystical theology known as Quietism.

Because Schopenhauer's theory of justice is an ontology, we need in addition to examine Schopenhauer's metaphysics proper. Curiously, although the Schopenhauerian view of justice is becoming increasingly relevant to today's jurisprudence, it is not an outgrowth of yesterday's jurisprudence. To some, that may be a disqualification. Others, however, tired of the endless journalized conversations among criticalists, economists, and civic republicans, not to mention liberals and conservatives, might find solace in Schopenhauer's almost-two-century-old "fresh" approach. Schopenhauer may even have something to say to those criticalists, economists, and civic republicans who still nurture the hope of finding a "unified field theory" in the multidimensional universe of jurisprudence, or at least a lingua franca in the juris-Babel of contemporary legal philosophies. The fact that Arthur Schopenhauer molded his amazingly prescient understanding of physical and metaphysical reality, that is to say, his ontology or study of being, into a theory of *justice*—a concept usually understood as belonging in the realm of ethics, or even epistemology or psychology, but hardly metaphysics or ontology—gives his philosophy surprising facets of uniqueness and scope.

Albert Einstein called Schopenhauer's writings "wonderful." Erwin Schrödinger called them "beautiful."[13] In this study, we may see what Erwin Schrödinger, Albert Einstein, and many others have seen in the writings of Arthur Schopenhauer. We are about to "experience the universe as a single significant whole." Enjoy the journey.

---

13. See Schrödinger, 110.

In Search of
Schopenhauer's Cat

Chapter 1

Schopenhauer's Life

An Incident

The year was 1840. The place, Copenhagen. The event, a meeting of the Danish Royal Society of the Sciences. The members of the Society found themselves in a quandary. They had sponsored a prize essay contest three years earlier and had invited submissions on the topic of "The Source and Foundation of Morals." It probably seemed to the Society to be an excellent moment in history for such a contest. Immanuel Kant had by that time been enshrined in the minds of European philosophers as the man who had at long last and perhaps even definitively established the rational and metaphysical foundations of morality. His work had by then been further systematized by Fichte, extended by Schelling, and explained by Hegel. It must have seemed, in 1837, as if a new "golden age" of speculative philosophy were dawning, and the Society's contest would, perhaps, serve to identify some budding and worthy successor to the mantle of Kant, Fichte, Schelling, and Hegel.

Alas, in the three years that had gone by since the announcement of the contest, only one lone contestant had submitted an entry. It was a lengthy essay written in German by a somewhat obscure scholar who at the time did not even hold an academic post. Those facts were not, however, the reasons for the Society's predicament. The trouble lay in the essay itself. The somewhat obscure scholar had referred to Kant's famed Categorical Imperative as "absurd moral pedantry," classified Fichte and Schelling as "philosophasters, dreamers, and visionaries," and called the revered Hegel (who had only recently suffered a tragic death in a cholera epidemic) a "clumsy and senseless charlatan." Then the essay went on to identify "compassion" as the source and foundation of morals.[1] Having rejected, in an anything-but-compassionate manner, Kant's account of the basis for morality and ethics, the essayist went on to embrace, quite heartily, Kant's "transcendental aesthetic"[2] and to argue from it to the conclusion that there is, at some unfathomable and unconscious level, a basic ontological oneness among human beings—a conclusion which he supported with references to the Vedanta of Hindu scripture. One can only imagine the perplexity of the members of the Society. After some delay, they decided not to award the prize at all.

The following year, Arthur Schopenhauer, the then obscure scholar whose essay had been rejected by the Society, published the document independently, under the title *On the Basis of Morality*,[3]

---

1. Arthur Schopenhauer, *On the Basis of Morality* (1841), trans. E. F. J. Payne (1965; rev. ed., Oxford: Berghahn Books, 1995), 66, 79, 80 (hereinafter, *Morality*).
2. See Immanuel Kant, *The Critique of Pure Reason* (1781 and 1787), trans. Norman Kemp Smith (New York: St. Martin's Press, 1965), 65–91 (hereinafter, Kant, *Pure Reason*). Essentially the term refers to Kant's doctrine of the ideality of space and time.
3. Schopenhauer joined *On the Basis of Morality* with another essay *On the Freedom of the Human Will* and published both under the title *The Two Fundamental Problems of Ethics*. The essay on the human will had been awarded a prize in a similar contest sponsored by the Scientific Society of Trondheim, Norway.

and took the occasion to excoriate the Society itself as "a league of journalists sworn to glorify the bad."[4] The indignity of losing a contest in which one's submission is the only entry might have explained the outburst as a momentary surrender to pique were it not for the fact that twenty years later, after his *Parerga and Paralipomena*[5] had secured his fame (and only a month before his death), Schopenhauer published a second edition of the essay and once again took the occasion to vilify the Society with implications that it was a suppressor of truth, a stifler of brains and talent, and a supporter of the fame of windbags and charlatans.[6] Schopenhauer, despite his immense capacity for taking and giving offense, indeed for wallowing in both, never seemed to understand why people would not take him seriously as the champion of compassion. Nor would he have understood how he could become, of all things, Adolf Hitler's favorite philosopher.[7]

It was not that Schopenhauer was blind to his own deficiencies in the area of compassion. He simply did not seem to understand why people should expect him to practice what he preached. He had a ready answer for those who would identify his personal views as sexist and anti-Semitic[8] and his outbursts as peevish, petty, and mali-

---

4. *Morality*, 14.
5. Schopenhauer, Arthur, *Parerga and Paralipomena* (1851), 2 vols., trans. E. F. J. Payne (Oxford: Clarendon Press, 1974) (hereinafter, *Parerga*).
6. *Morality*, 33.
7. See, e.g., Robert Payne, *The Life and Death of Adolf Hitler* (New York: Praeger, 1973), 115 (hereinafter, Payne); John Toland, *Adolf Hitler* (Garden City, N.Y.: Doubleday, 1976), 1: 85 (hereinafter, Toland); and Joachim C. Fest, *Hitler*, trans. Richard and Clara Winston (New York: Harcourt Brace Janovich, 1974), 69, 200 (hereinafter, Fest).
8. See Arthur Schopenhauer, *Essays and Aphorisms*, trans. R. J. Hollingdale (Middlesex: Penguin Books, 1970), 80–88 (hereinafter, *Essays*), for a sampling of his views on women. Joachim Fest, the journalist and biographer of Hitler, writes of Nietzsche acknowledging Schopenhauer's "hatred of the Jews." Fest, 56. Also, Hitler himself once quoted Schopenhauer as referring to the Jew as "the great master in lying." Adolf Hitler, *Mein Kampf* (1927), trans. Ralph Manheim (Boston: Houghton Mifflin, 1971), 305.

cious. Schopenhauer seemed to recognize his vulnerability on many a moral score when he wrote, in his magnum opus:

> It is ... just as little necessary for the saint to be a philosopher as for the philosopher to be a saint; just as it is not necessary for a perfectly beautiful person to be a great sculptor, or for a great sculptor to be himself a beautiful person. In general, it is a strange demand on a moralist that he should commend no other virtue than that which he himself possesses.[9]

There is something fascinating about a self-proclaimed champion of compassion who vilifies his colleagues and holds grudges for decades. Philosophers usually purport to practice what they preach. Schopenhauer makes no such pretension, and that makes him a rarity. His claim on us, then, is not in his emotings but rather in his theory. Some of us will no doubt suggest that his life gives the lie to his theory. But to others of us, perhaps, the real fascination in the saga of Schopenhauer lies in surmising why his own theory seemed to have no personal claim on him. There are reasons.

A Curriculum Vitae

Character looms large in Schopenhauer's thought. He believed that character is "the real core of the whole man" and that it is "inborn."[10] Arthur Schopenhauer's already inborn character first saw the light of day on February 22, 1788, in what is now Gdansk, Poland.[11]

The Schopenhauer family was wealthy and well connected, and

---

9. Arthur Schopenhauer, *The World as Will and Representation* (1819), vol. 1, trans. E. F. J. Payne (New York: Dover Books, 1969), 383 (hereinafter, *WWR*-1).
10. Arthur Schopenhauer, *On the Freedom of the Will* (1841), trans. Konstantin Kolenda (Indianapolis: Bobbs-Merrill, 1960), 56 (hereinafter, *Freedom*).
11. For further information on Schopenhauer's life, see Rüdiger Safranski,

seems to have had a cosmopolitan propensity for travel and for language. One of the reasons why the name Arthur was chosen, it is said, was that his mother favored it because it was spelled the same in German, French, and English. By the time he was a teenager Arthur had already developed a fluency in all three languages. Until the college years, Arthur's education was anything but conventional. He seems to have been brought up on French literature and other fashionable readings of the day. From boyhood, under the influence of his father, he read *The Times* (London) daily.

Despite the intellectual stimulation in his early upbringing, the young Schopenhauer did not find himself sliding easily into the life of a scholar and a philosopher. His father expected him to come into the family business and consistently discouraged any deeper academic ambitions. In fact, at the age of seventeen, Arthur actually gave up schooling altogether and went to work in his father's office. Shortly thereafter, however, an event occurred that was pivotal in the young man's life. The family was living in Hamburg at the time, and his father had been going through episodes of depression and mood swings. One morning, the elder Schopenhauer's body was found floating in the canal near his place of business, and of course suicide was suspected. In later life, as a philosopher, Schopenhauer would deal sensitively and somewhat ambivalently with the topic of suicide.[12]

The death of his father affected the young Schopenhauer deeply, but perhaps more important to any analysis of the depth of Schopen-

---

Schopenhauer and the Wild Years of Philosophy, trans. Ewald Osers (Cambridge: Harvard University Press, 1990) (hereinafter, Safranski); V. J. McGill, *Schopenhauer: Pessimist and Pagan* (New York: Brentano's, 1931); Helen Zimmern, *Schopenhauer: His Life and Philosophy* (London: Longmans Green, 1876); Frederick Copleston, S.J., *Arthur Schopenhauer: Philosopher of Pessimism* (Andover, Hants, U.K.: Burns, Oates & Washbourne, 1946), 18–44 (hereinafter, Copleston); and Magee, 3–27.

12. See, e.g., *WWR*-1, at 398–99. See also *Essays,* at 77–79. But see *Parerga,* vol. 2, ch. 13, 307–11.

hauer's pessimism was the effect that his father's death had upon his mother. It seems to have liberated her. Shortly after the death of her spouse, she left young Arthur in Hamburg and moved to Weimar, where she proceeded to become a novelist of international renown.

It is in the curious relationship between Schopenhauer and his mother that one can perhaps more easily find the roots of the pessimism and the peevishness, pettiness, and paranoia that infected him as an adult and that tainted much, though not all, of his work. Johanna Schopenhauer has been described as easygoing and party loving in social situations, but also as brittle and unfeeling in private life, and Arthur undoubtedly suffered from maternal deprivation and from the inconsistency between his mother's public and private personalities. One oft-recounted incident in Schopenhauer's life well illustrates his relationship with his mother. At the age of nineteen, Schopenhauer resumed his academic career, and six years later he received his doctorate in philosophy from the University of Jena. Proudly, one might imagine, he presented a copy of his recently published doctoral dissertation, entitled *On the Fourfold Root of the Principle of Sufficient Reason* (even today regarded as a minor philosophical classic), to his mother. Her response was to remark that a book called the fourfold "root" of something or other must be intended for apothecaries. The proud young doctor of philosophy, angry and hurt, countered with the statement that his book would still be available when all the novels she was publishing were long forgotten. She agreed, and added that the entire first printing of his book would indeed still be available.[13] For virtually his entire adult life Schopenhauer was in a competitive, hostile relationship with his mother.

If there was a time in Schopenhauer's life that could be considered formative it probably was those years of 1813 and 1814 when the competitiveness and hostility in the mother/son relationship

---

13. See Magee, 10.

were moulding his character, and when something else was also occurring, simultaneously. There are indeed two strains in Schopenhauer's thought: the base, opinionated emotings and the profound, almost prophetic understandings of the human condition. The emotings can, perhaps, be traced to his problems in relating to his mother, but those problems can only partially, if at all, explain the genesis of the deeper aspects of his theory. The other set of events that was occurring in 1813 and 1814 was that Schopenhauer was falling into protégé relationships with two older scholars. One was none other than the immortal Goethe. The other was a far less celebrated figure, an oriental scholar named Friedrich Majer. Curiously, it was Majer, rather than Goethe, whose influence on Schopenhauer's thought proved to be the more lasting. Majer introduced Schopenhauer to the great philosophies of the East, Hinduism and Buddhism. By the time he had met Majer, Schopenhauer had already published *On the Fourfold Root of the Principle of Sufficient Reason,* which was deeply Kantian in vocabulary and tone. What ignited Schopenhauer's mind at the time he met Majer was the recognition that, while working entirely within the Western, Kantian tradition, he had arrived at philosophical positions that were central to Eastern thought.[14]

This has always been one of the reasons why Schopenhauer's philosophy is so fascinating. He formed its initial postulates based solely on his acquaintance with the Western philosophical tradition (steeped heavily in Platonism and Kantianism) and found them largely confirmed in the Eastern Hindu and Buddhist traditions.

Five years after the publication of his doctoral thesis, Schopenhauer published his magnum opus, *Die Welt als Wille und Vorstellung,* that is, *The World as Will and Representation.*[15] Schopenhauer

---

14. Magee, 15.
15. The first translators of Schopenhauer's book into English, R. B. Haldane and J. Kemp, rendered its title as *The World as Will and Idea.* It is understandable that

was thirty years old at the time he wrote the first edition of *The World as Will and Representation,* and he expected that the work would establish him as a well-recognized scholar and philosopher. Instead, it met with public and professional apathy. In a sense, the fact that Schopenhauer's masterwork did not generate wide acceptance and approbation determined the course of the rest of his writings. Everything of consequence that Schopenhauer wrote from that day on can fairly be described as an effort to further and better explain the thesis that he put forth in *The World as Will and Representation.*

Two years after the publication of his magnum opus, however, Schopenhauer did achieve a university lectureship at the University of Berlin. His great nemesis Hegel was, at the time, also lecturing at Berlin and was, moreover, at the height of his personal fame. The fledgling lecturer Schopenhauer characteristically scheduled his own lectures to be given at the same time as Hegel's. When no one came, legend has it that Schopenhauer lectured to an empty

---

they chose in their 1883 work to translate *"Vorstellung"* as "Idea." The word *"Vorstellung"* had been widely used in *German* philosophy as a translation of Locke's *English* term "idea," and Schopenhauer did use the term in that Lockean sense. *"Vorstellung"* literally refers to "something put before" or a "presentation," and in context can easily convey the sense of "idea." Some further confusion is generated by reason of the fact that Schopenhauer had a special and limited place for his understanding of the Platonic "Idea" in a portion of his metaphysics. Wherever Schopenhauer wrote of the Platonic Idea, however, he used the German word *"Idee,"* never *"Vorstellung."* E. J. F. Payne translated the book anew into English in 1958 and decided not to stay with the word "idea" for *"Vorstellung";* he gave the word *"Vorstellung"* what he felt was the more accurate translation of "representation." Of course the word "representation" has several meanings and nuances. As Payne used the term, the word carries the very literal meaning of "re-presentation," i.e., "presentation again." As Payne, understands it, Schopenhauer's main thesis is that the world "presents" itself to our organ of perception, but our organ of perception imposes the concepts of space and time and the principle of causality on it and then re-presents it, i.e., presents it anew, to us. It may well be, however, that Schopenhauer did not have this "re-presenting" sense in his use of "Vorstellung." He may simply have been referencing what is "presented," not "re-presented," i.e., a function of the understanding. The world, according to Schopenhauer, is "will" and is also "a function of understanding." See Magee, 109.

room, and apocryphal or not, such a response would have been typical of the haughty stubbornness in the character of the philosopher. What is clear is that when the choice of changing his schedule or abandoning his course was pressed upon him, Schopenhauer simply chose to abandon his career as a university lecturer, never to return. He spent virtually the entire rest of his life (almost forty years) studying and writing.

That is not to say that the rest of Schopenhauer's life was uneventful or unproductive. In 1821 he met and subsequently had a five-year love affair with a young woman named Caroline Richter (Medon) and was alleged to have fathered her child, a son whom she named Carl Ludwig Gustav Medon. Schopenhauer, however never acknowledged the boy, and there is no credible evidence that Schopenhauer was the boy's father. Schopenhauer did, however, specifically exclude the boy, by name, from his last will and testament. Despite his negativity towards the boy, Schopenhauer remained emotionally attached to Caroline, although not she to him, for the rest of his life. He was also involved in a lengthy episode of litigation. Another woman named Caroline, Caroline Marquet, sued him after he bodily threw her out of the anteroom to his apartment. After more than a decade of trials and appeals, she eventually won, and Schopenhauer was forced to pay her a disability maintenance award for the rest of her life, which amounted to twenty-six years. Upon the woman's death, Schopenhauer penned a memorial epithet in Latin: *"Obit anus, abit onus"* (The old woman has died; the burden has been lifted).[16]

---

16. The story of the two Carolines is told in greater detail in the Rüdiger Safranski biography of Schopenhauer. See Safranski, 269–73. As to the Latin epithet, Schrödinger has Schopenhauer writing it in his diary, but Magee has him scrawling it across a copy of the woman's death certificate. See Copleston, 33; Schrödinger, 109; Magee, 13 n. Both Magee and Copleston report the Latin inscription as *"obit anus, abit onus."* Schrödinger reports it as *"obiit anus, abiit onus."* Whatever version

In terms of productivity in those years, there were, of course, the prize essay contests—the 1839 Trondheim, Norway, contest which he won, and the 1840 Danish contest which he lost (even though his entry was the lone submission)—and the amplified second volume of his masterwork, *Die Welt als Wille und Vorstellung*, in 1844.

Schopenhauer died on September 21, 1860, at the age of seventy-two. Until the 1850s he was a virtual unknown to the general public. It was not until the publication of his *Parerga and Paralipomena* (a collection of philosophical essays and aphorisms)[17] in 1851 that fame and recognition crept into his life in his declining years. The agent that brought fame and recognition, however, was not his *Parerga and Paralipomena*—at least not directly. In April of 1853, a scholar named John Oxenford published an article entitled "Iconoclasm in German Philosophy" in the *Westminster Review* in England. The article understandably highlighted Schopenhauer, who might be regarded as the Iconoclast of Iconoclasts. The popularity of the article created a demand for translations of Schopenhauer's works into English, and ignited an interest in those works not only in Great Britain, but on the Continent as well.[18] And in those last few years, Schopenhauer basked in the recognition, appreciation, and indeed lionization that he knew he had deserved all along.

Schopenhauer may have used, the version of Schrödinger, the quantum physicist (rather than Magee the philosopher's or Copleston the Jesuit priest-philosopher's), is interestingly more correct in terms of Latin grammar. *"Obivit"* (or in its contracted form *"obiit"*) is the third person singular, perfect tense form of the verb "obire," meaning "to die." *"Abiit"* is the third person singular, perfect tense form of the verb *"abire,"* meaning "to go away."

17. The title means "complementary works and matters omitted." Christopher Janaway, *Schopenhauer* (Oxford: Oxford University Press, 1994), 10.

18. The article was translated into German and published in the *Vossische Zeitung*, and a similar article with a similar effect was published also in France. See Copleston, 40–41.

Chapter 2

Kant's Influence

At its core, Schopenhauer's theory of knowledge (and ultimately his ontological theory of justice) is deeply metaphysical and deeply Kantian. It has its starting point, indeed its essential grounding, in the basic premise of Immanuel Kant's own theory of knowledge—a premise which Kant himself referred to as his own "Copernican Revolution."

Kant's great "Copernican" discovery was that the world of our experience must, if it is to be perceived by us, conform to the patterns of our perceiving instrument. According to Kant, we do not see the world as it is, but rather as our mind structures it for us. Just as Copernicus had hypothesized that apparent astronomical motion, for example, the sun moving across the sky, is really found in the observer's local frame of reference rather than in the intrinsic motion of the heavenly body, so too, Kant hypothesized that many of the constituents of nature, for example, time, space, and causality, are really found in the observer's local frame of reference rather than in the intrinsic nature of things. We see things in time and space and we perceive things as adhering to the principle of cause and effect, not because the things and the events in themselves impose time, space, and causality on our perceiving instrument, that is, the mind, but because the very structure of the mind imposes time, space, and causality on our perceptions of the things and events. About things as they really are in themselves, according to Kant, we can know nothing. As Kant himself put it,

> [h]itherto it has been assumed that all our knowledge must conform to objects. But all attempts to extend our knowledge of objects by establishing something in regard to them a priori, by means of concepts, have, on this assumption, ended in failure. We must therefore make trial whether we may not have more success in the tasks of metaphysics, if we suppose that objects must conform to our knowledge. . . . We should then be proceeding on the lines of Copernicus' primary hypothesis. Failing of satisfactory progress in explaining the movements of the heavenly bodies on the supposition that they all revolved round the spectator, he tried whether he might not have better success if he made the spectator to revolve and the stars to remain at rest.[1]

Kant's tenets about the structure of the perceiving mind conditioning in some way the perception of outside reality to such an extent that we can never get a clear grasp on what that outside reality is *in itself,* have filtered down into one of the main tenets of quantum physics, the Heisenberg uncertainty principle. In quantum theory, the very act of observation (Kant might say "the structure of the perceiving mind") changes what is observed. Werner Heisenberg him-

---

1. Kant, *Pure Reason*, xvi–xvii, 22.

self drew the decidedly Kantian conclusion that "We cannot know, as a matter of principle, the present [the thing-in-itself, in Kantian terms] in all its details."[2] It is difficult to find a popular study of quantum physics that does *not* cite Kant's theory of knowledge, with Kant's own "uncertainty principle." While Heisenberg himself acknowledged that Kant's notion of the a priori ideality of space, time, and causality (i.e., Kant's positioning of those entities in the structure of the perceiving mind) is "no longer contained in the scientific system of modern physics," he went on to say: "Still Kant's views on the positioning of those entities form an essential part of this system in a somewhat different sense.... Modern physics has changed Kant's statement about the possibility of synthetic judgments a priori from a metaphysical one into a practical one."[3] The point seems to be that modern physics has done, to some extent at least, what Kant thought impossible, that is, learn something true and accurate about the "thing-in-itself" behind or beneath phenomenal reality, but at the practical, experimental level, that "something," though knowable, is plagued with uncertainty. Heisenberg, throughout his book on *Physics and Philosophy*, never mentioned Schopenhauer. His philosophical references stopped with Kant. But the implication of his conclusion that, contrary to Kant, something (albeit something plagued with uncertainty) *can* be known about deep reality, that is, the thing-in-itself, is that Schopenhauer was correct in reaching the same conclusion.

It is understandable and completely justifiable that Kant himself should liken his discovery of a new metaphysical vantage point to the astronomical discovery made by Copernicus. Kant was a prolific

---

2. Quoted in John Gribben, *Q is for Quantum: Particle Physics from A to Z*, s.v. "uncertainty principle" (London: Weidenfeld & Nicholson, 1998), 418.
3. Werner Heisenberg, *Physics and Philosophy: The Revolution in Modern Science* (1958) (Amherst, N.Y.: Prometheus Books (1999), 90–91.

and prodigious scholar in many disciplines, and his own accomplishments in the science of astronomy are still to this day regarded as monumental. For example, Kant has a genuine claim to have been the first to establish scientifically that the Milky Way is a mass of disparate stars and to apply that insight to the elliptical nebulae, regarding them as distant mass systems of disparate stars.[4]

This tenet that the very structure of our mind imposes time, space, and causality on our perceptions of the things and events that we are encountering was the underpinning of Kant's theory of knowledge, and Schopenhauer accepted it wholeheartedly—but only to a point. Recall Kant's main conclusion: About things as they really are in themselves we can know nothing. Schopenhauer claimed that there *is* a way in which we can know *something* about things as they really are *in themselves,* that is, stripped of the time, space, causality, and other impedimenta imposed by the structure of the perceiving mind.

Kant divided his theory of knowledge, with its revolutionary Copernican twist, into what he called the "transcendental aesthetic" and the "transcendental logic," based roughly on the distinction between knowledge through sense perception and knowledge through applied reasoning.[5] To the former he relegated space and time, as *conditions* of sensation, that is, prerequisites *for* sensation, imposed by the perceiving subject on the perceived object in order to make it intelligible. To the latter he relegated the principle of causality and eleven other "categories" of pure thought. Schopenhauer, however,

---

4. See Charles A. Whitney, *The Discovery of Our Galaxy* (New York: Alfred A. Knopf, 1971), 83–86. There is another thing that Copernicus's astronomical vantage point and Kant's metaphysical vantage point have in common. Both were, in a sense, not discoveries, but rather rediscoveries. Copernicus's heliocentric model had been anticipated by Aristarchus of Samos in the third century, B.C., and Kant's positing that objects must conform to our knowledge has its ancient analogue in Plato's Theory of Ideas.

5. See Kant, *Pure Reason*, A19–A22, B34–B36, 65–67.

jettisoned eleven of Kant's categories of pure thought, retaining in his metaphysics only the category of causality, along with time and space, and regarding it, as did Kant, as a condition of pure thought, an imposition of the structure of the perceiving mind.

Kant's "Copernican Revolution," that is, his thesis that those properties and characteristics that we commonly think of as inhering in objects and events in themselves, for example, space, time, and causality, are in reality inherent in the structure of the mind of the perceiving subject, was brilliantly responsive to the philosophical problems of his age. Kant's innovation answered the skepticism of Hume by preserving the reality (albeit an unknowable reality) of the objective world while at the same time avoiding the extreme subjective idealism of Berkeley.

In framing his response, however, Kant had created a problem. His brilliant insight flew in the face of the Scientific Enlightenment, premised as it was on the ability to know objects-in-themselves with certainty and reliability. Consequently it was, perhaps, predictable that the philosophers who followed Kant roughly divided themselves into two camps: (1) those who sought ways out of the Kantian dilemma in efforts to save the certainty and reliability of the knowledge of objects-in-themselves, typified by Hegel (who sought to link the structure of the perceiving mind with the perceived object by identifying the movements of thought with pulsations of real being),[6] and (2) those who accepted the Kantian dilemma wholeheartedly and made efforts to explore it more deeply, typified by Schopenhauer.

This thesis of Kant's—that we perceive things as adhering to the principle of cause and effect, and as existing in time and space, *not* because the things-in-themselves actually *do* adhere to the principle of cause and effect and actually *do* exist in time and space, but rather

---

6. See, e.g., James Collins, *A History of Modern European Philosophy* (Milwaukee: Bruce Publishing Company, 1954), 604–6.

because the very structure of the perceiving mind imposes causality, time, and space on our perceptions of the things—is all-important to an understanding of Schopenhauer's metaphysics. Schopenhauer accepted it for the brilliant insight that it was, and it is not inaccurate to say that he based his entire metaphysics on it. For Schopenhauer as for Kant, human beings prior to all experience (a priori) know the law of causality. Indeed, it is the *condition* of experience itself. It is the sieve through which experience must be drained in order for us to be aware of it. It is the form which experience must take in order to reach our consciousness. It is the binary code into which experience must by put in order to be processable. Our consciousness is structured in such a way that it can only process experience in accordance with the cause-and-effect code. The computer analogy may not sit well with many of us, but it is apt in describing Schopenhauer's thought. In part (but *only* in part), Schopenhauer's world is indeed as deterministic as the world the computer would perceive, if it had consciousness.

To others, even to other Kantians, Kant's thesis was something of a stumbling block, perhaps even an embarrassment. If accepted at face value, it seemed to make impossible any metaphysics at all. The word "metaphysics" is usually understood as meaning an inquiry into the ultimate nature of things, the ultimate nature of reality. Indeed, the conclusion that Kant himself drew from his thesis—that is, the conclusion that we can know nothing about things as they are *in themselves*—seemed to deny even the possibility of a metaphysical inquiry as that term is usually understood.

Hegel chose one way of resolving the dilemma raised by Kant's thesis, and Schopenhauer another. In a sense, Hegel's resolution of the dilemma was probably closer to Kant's own implicit resolution of it. If the structure of our own perceiving mind is the thing that imposes space, time, and causality on the external world, then that is all we have to go on. Regardless of what things are truly like *in themselves*, we have only the rationality that our perceiving minds superimpose on them. That rationality *is* the reality in that sense, the only one we can deal with. Hence Hegel's famous statement: "The real is the rational and the rational is the real."

Schopenhauer saw that as shallow and simplistic—more of a refusal to deal with Kant's brilliant insight than an exploration and explication of it. Schopenhauer's resolution of the dilemma differed from Hegel's. He accepted Kant's thesis, but not the conclusion that Kant drew from it.

Chapter 3

Schopenhauer's Departure from Kant

Schopenhauer agreed with Kant that our perceiving mind is the thing that imposes time, space, and causality on external things. He disagreed, however, with Kant's lament that we cannot know anything about external things as they are in themselves. In Schopenhauer's view we *can* know something about external things as they are *in themselves*.[1] We *can* know something about the *ultimate nature* of reality. This is true, reasoned Schopenhauer, because we have the ability to view ourselves from, as it were, *two* vantage points. Kant never took this fully into account, according to Schopenhauer. The relationship that we have with all the rest of the world is one of subject (our perceiving mind) *to* object (everything out there in the external world). But as to our *selves*, we are both subject *and* object, *and we know it*. We have a simultaneous dual insight into our own nature. We can view our selves as perceiving subjects and as perceived objects. This simultaneous dual insight has an immediacy to

---

1. Schopenhauer would not use the term "things in themselves" in the plural. As we shall see, for Schopenhauer, ultimate reality is singular and unindividuated; it is "will."

it that allows us to prescind from the impositions of the perceiving mind and to experience the non-dualistic unity that we think of as our *selves*. And when we do this—when we strip away time, space, causality, and even individuation itself and try to get a direct and immediate understanding of what is left—we do find something— something like a tendency to exist or a tendency to act. If we were to give this something—this tendency to exist and to act—a name, we would be hard pressed to call it anything but a "will." And that is the word Schopenhauer chose.

The perceiving mind, when it engages in this dual insight, recognizes itself as both subject and object, and tries to understand itself as a non-dualistic unity, finds that it is, at base, "will." As Hegel identified "rationality" as the ultimate reality, Schopenhauer identified "will." Moreover, as Hegel found "rationality" in all existing things, so too Schopenhauer found "will." In each case, of course, the terms chosen were problematic approximations. Stones do not "think" any more than they "will." Schopenhauer explains:

> [T]he knowledge everyone has of his own *willing* . . . is neither a perception (for all perception is spatial), nor is it empty; on the contrary, it is more real than any other knowledge. . . . [O]ur willing . . . is the one thing known to us *immediately*, and not given to us merely in the representation, as all else is. Here, therefore, lies . . . the only narrow gateway to truth. Accordingly, we must learn to understand nature from ourselves, not ourselves from nature. . . . [I]f all other phenomena could be known by us just as immediately and intimately, we should be obliged to regard them precisely as that which the will is in us. Therefore in this sense I teach that the inner nature of everything is *will*, and I call the will the thing-in-itself.[2]

2. *WWR*-2, 196–97 (emphasis in original).

Schopenhauer's inconspicuous statement that "we must learn to understand nature from ourselves, not ourselves from nature" can be viewed, at least with respect to the Western philosophy of his day, as his own little "Copernican Revolution."[3]

"Will," if it is the thing-in-itself not only of the human being, but also of all other things, cannot stand as what we usually take it to signify—a decision-making organ. And indeed, in Schopenhauer's thought, it does not mean that. At one point in his magnum opus, Schopenhauer identified "will" with the *forma substantialis* of the scholastics, and cited the great Catholic philosopher Francisco Suarez.[4] At another point, he described what this "will" would be like in, of all things, a stone—and cited Spinoza in the bargain:

> Spinoza (*Epist.* 62) says that if a stone projected through the air had consciousness, it would imagine it was flying of its own will. I add merely that the stone would be right. The impulse is for it what motive is for me, and what in the case of the stone appears as cohesion, gravitation, rigidity in the assumed condition, is by its inner nature, the same as what I recognize in myself as will, and which the stone would also recognize as will, if knowledge were added in its case also.[5]

"Will" for the stone is simply the tendency to be what it is—the tendency not to decompose, or turn into something else, or vanish from existence. Schopenhauer chose the word "will" to describe this principle of reality undoubtedly because, starting from Kant's transcen-

---

3. Schopenhauer himself referred to that "inconspicuous statement" as "my revolutionary principle." *Schopenhauer Manuscript Remains,* vol. 1 (Berg, 1988), para. 621.
4. *WWR*-1, 123.
5. *WWR*-1, 126. What may perhaps be a more Spinozistic viewpoint on the same topic appears in Annie Dillard, *Teaching a Stone to Talk: Expeditions and Encounters* (New York: Harper, 1982), 69.

dental aesthetic and transcendental logic,[6] he found it first in the human being. One might easily surmise that had his approach allowed him to start at the level of inanimate things (as the approach of today's quantum physicists allows), he likely would have chosen a word like "tendency" rather than "will."

The end result of this departure from Kant's paralyzing conclusion that reality in itself is unknowable is Schopenhauer's basic metaphysical thesis. It is easily stated; in fact, it is quite simply the title of his masterwork: *The World as Will and Representation*.[7] Reality in itself, the ground of all being, is *"will,"* and we perceive this "will" in the world not directly, but rather in a second-hand fashion. Our minds restructure this "will" and *re-present* it to our consciousnesses wrapped in the concepts of time and space and in the principle of causality. The world *is* "will" and *is also* "re-presentation."

In his "Copernican Revolution," Kant had shown that the phenomenal world (i.e., the immediate, apparent world) is conditioned at least as much by the perceiver (the subject) as by that which is perceived (the object). What Schopenhauer did was to focus more intently on the phenomenal world as being "representation" (re-presentation), and to identify the inner nature of the object (the thing-in-itself)—and the inner nature of the subject too—as "will." Kant would have agreed with the first half of the preceding sentence, that is, that the phenomenal world is re-presentation; in effect, that statement is simply a restatement of Kant's "Copernican Revolution." Kant, however, stopped there. Kant had concluded that we could never actually know the inner, essential, real nature of the world out there, that is to say, the thing-in-itself. Schopenhauer's claim is that he has found a route whereby the human mind can actually come to know the thing-in-itself, reality as it truly is in itself, and not simply

---

6. Kant, *Pure Reason*, xvi–xvii, 22.
7. Magee, 19.

"reality" as it is restructured and represented to our consciousness through the structures of our minds. The means of access to this route lies in the fact that there is one "object" that is not represented to us through the structure of our perceiving instrument, one "object" of which our consciousness can have direct, unmediated experience—itself. When this route is taken, our consciousness experiences itself, its own inner nature, as "will":

> To the subject of knowing, who appears as an individual only through his identity with the body, this body is given in two entirely different ways. It is given in intelligent perception as representation, as an object among objects, liable to the laws of these objects. But it is also given in quite a different way, namely as what is known immediately to everyone, and is denoted by the word *will*. Every true act of his will is also at once and inevitably a movement of his body; he cannot actually will the act without at the same time being aware that it appears as a movement of his body. The act of will and the action of the body are not two different states objectively known, connected by the bond of causality; they do not stand in the relation of cause and effect, but are one and the same thing, though given in two entirely different ways, first quite directly, and then in perception for the understanding. The action of the body is nothing but the act of the will objectified, i.e., translated into perception.[8]

The point here is that we see our bodies and their movements as subject to the principle of cause and effect, but we also have a direct experience of what our perceiving instrument (i.e., our minds) represent to us as the *cause* of the movement, and we experience this as an act of our *will*. We *willed* to raise our arm, to turn our glance, to stand

8. *WWR*-1, 100.

up, to sit down, and it happened. And that raising of the arm, and so on, is experienced within us as *will.* When we try to analyze the event, our mind, because it is structured to do so, invariably presents the willing as the *cause* of the movement, but there is also the direct experience of that event as a wanting, a desiring, a needing, a choosing, and in more serious contexts a craving. That direct experience is, Schopenhauer posited, a direct experience of the *thing-in-itself,* unmediated by the impositions of the structure of our mind. Moreover, that act of will and that action of the body are not two different states objectively known, connected by the bond of causality. Our mind imposes the causality. The willing and the action do not stand in the relation of cause and effect. They are one and the same thing, though given in two entirely different ways: the willing is given quite directly, and then the action is given in perception for the understanding. Schopenhauer thus claimed to have found a way around the metaphysical roadblock that Kant's "Copernican Revolution" seemed to have introduced. We *can* have a direct experience, and therefore knowledge at least to some degree, of the thing-in-itself.

The Kantian Flaw

Schopenhauer did more than simply trek out on his own, metaphysically speaking. He claimed to have discovered a major flaw in Kant's thinking—a flaw that made the logic of Kant's position one of pure subjective idealism. Pure subjective idealism would hold that the world out there is something like an imaginary projection and that it does not really exist at all outside the subject's mind. Kant explicitly rejected pure subjective idealism, but Schopenhauer insisted that Kant's position logically led to it.

In his *Critique of Pure Reason,* Kant had refuted Berkeley's pure subjective idealism by arguing that our "inner experience . . . is possible only on the assumption of outer experience."⁹ In other words, there *must* be something out there causing whatever perceptions we have of it. In essence, this would seem to be an unremarkable use of the principle of cause and effect. But recall, argued Schopenhauer, that Kant in his "Copernican Revolution" had declared that the principle of cause and effect was of *subjective* origin. One can only draw the conclusion that the world out there *causes* experiences in the subject by granting *objective* significance to the principle of causality.

Schopenhauer reasoned that Kant himself may have recognized and become alarmed by the subjective idealist implications of his theory and that that was a major reason why Kant published a revised edition of his *Critique of Pure Reason* only six years after the publication of the original. In truth, it does seem that in the original *Critique* Kant wanders into some strange statements for one who views himself as *refuting* the idealism of Berkeley. For example, "it is clearly shown that if I remove the thinking subject the whole corporeal world must at once vanish; it is nothing save an appearance in the sensibility of our subject and a mode of its representation."¹⁰ It is not insignificant that Kant left that statement out of the revised edition. In truth, however, the logic of Kant's early position (if one can excuse the statement from it, quoted above) seems more like Descartes's "problematic" idealism (the doctrine that the existence of objects outside our minds is merely doubtful and indemonstrable) than the pure subjective idealism of Berkeley (which Kant referred to as "*dogmatic* idealism").¹¹

Schopenhauer's recent biographer, Rüdiger Safranski, has sug-

---

9. Kant, *Pure Reason*, 244. The quoted language is taken somewhat out of context, but it does express the gist of Kant's thesis, which appears on p. 245. Kant put it this way: "The mere, but empirically determined, consciousness of my own experience proves the existence of objects in space outside me."
10. Kant, *Pure Reason* (1st ed., 1781), 354.
11. Kant, *Pure Reason*, 244 (emphasis in original).

gested that the discovery of the "Kantian flaw" should rightly be credited to Gottlob Ernst Schulze, Schopenhauer's philosophy teacher at Göttingen University, rather than to Schopenhauer. Schulze's discovery informed Johann Gottlieb Fichte (whose lectures Schopenhauer had attended as a young man):

> Fichte, basing himself on Schopenhauer's Göttingen philosophy teacher Gottlob Ernst Schulze . . . had discovered a faulty derivation of "thing in itself" by Kant [wrote Safranski]. He argued like this: The assumption that the world, as it appeared to us was concealing a world as it was in itself, and this world-in-itself as "material" was ultimately the *cause* of what, by means of our senses and reason, we would transform into the phenomenal world—this, as it were, "realistic" assumption was itself made by means of the causality principle, i.e., by means of our intellect. In other words, the causality principle, which was valid only for the phenomenal world, was being applied to a sphere that lay beyond appearance. . . . (Schopenhauer was subsequently to adopt this argument against Kant.)[12]

In his turn, and perhaps characteristically, Schopenhauer addressed Fichte's handling of the Kantian flaw in a scathingly negative manner:

> The great defect of the Kantian system in this point [wrote Schopenhauer], which, as I have said, was soon demonstrated, is an illustration of the beautiful Indian proverb: "No lotus without a stem." Here the stem is the faulty deduction of the thing-in-itself, though only the method of deduction, not the recognition of a thing-in-itself belonging to the given phenomenon. But

---

12. Safranski, 126.

in this last way Fichte misunderstood it, and this was possible only because he was concerned not with truth, but with making a sensation for the furtherance of his personal ends. Accordingly, he was foolhardy and thoughtless enough altogether to deny the thing-in-itself, and to set up a system in which not the merely formal part of the representation, as with Kant, but also the material, namely its whole content, was ostensibly deduced a priori from the subject. He quite correctly reckoned here on the public's lack of judgement and stupidity, for they accepted wretched sophisms, mere hocus-pocus, and senseless twaddle as proofs, so that he succeeded in turning the public's attention from Kant to himself, and in giving to German philosophy the direction in which it was after-wards carried by Schelling, finally reaching its goal in the senseless sham wisdom of Hegel.[13]

Stripped of its scathing negativity, what Schopenhauer was suggesting was that there is indeed a "Kantian flaw." Kant, in his effort to prove the existence of the deep-down thing-in-itself noumenal level of reality, did indeed use the principle of causation, which operates according to Kant's own philosophy only at the level of the world of phenomena and *not* at the level of the deep down, thing-in-itself, noumenal level. That flaw in Kant's thinking led Fichte and others to deny the existence of any thing-in-itself (by implication bringing them very close to Berkeleyian "dogmatic" idealism). Schopenhauer, however, says that Kant's only mistake was in using an improper method of proving the existence of the deep-down thing-in-itself noumenal level of reality. In other words, Schopenhauer is saying that the deep down, thing-in-itself, noumenal level of reality does exist, and its existence can be proven, or at least reasoned to, but not by Kant's method, that is, not by using the principle of causality.

13. *WWR*-1, 436–37.

Chapter 4

Schopenhauer's Own Claim to Fame

Schopenhauer was not being picky in arguing the existence of this flaw in Kant's theory. The flaw, if indeed it is one, exists at a very important point in the web of Kant's reasoning, the point at which subject touches object and object touches subject. If indeed it is a flaw, and more importantly, if Schopenhauer's own theory rectifies the flaw and fills the gap, then Schopenhauer's claim to greatness has undoubted merit.

There is a difficulty in explaining how it is that Schopenhauer tries to fill the gap between subject and object, between perceiver and outside world. He doesn't use any one, single principle, and the filling agents that he does use are, to some extent, outside the Western view of things. First of all, there is no doubt that Schopenhauer saw the issue clearly: "[I]t is ultimately the reality or ideality of matter which is the point in question.... Among the moderns only Locke has asserted positively and straightforwardly the reality of matter.... Berkeley alone has denied matter positively and without modifications."[1] From his posing of the issue in this manner, one

1. *WWR*-2, 12.

might expect Schopenhauer to claim some sort of middle ground, but instead (and surprisingly to our Western minds), he claims what might be fairly called an "all-ground," or perhaps a transcendent ground:

> The fundamental mistake of all systems is the failure to recognize this truth, namely that *the intellect and matter are correlatives,* in other words, the one exists only for the other; both stand and fall together; the one is only the other's reflex. They are in fact really one and the same thing, considered from two opposite points of view; and this one thing . . . is the phenomenon of the will or of the thing-in-itself.[2]

This is a difficult statement for our Western minds. Western minds like to classify and categorize. One tendency that some might have on reading the above statement would be to conclude that Schopenhauer was a pure subjective idealist: Matter *is* intellect. Another tendency that others might have would be to conclude, with equal vigor, that Schopenhauer was a materialist: Intellect *is* matter. Still others, perhaps, might conclude that Schopenhauer was unjustifiably adopting both inconsistent views.

To the Eastern mind, however, Schopenhauer's position would probably seem somewhat clearer and certainly more defensible. The Eastern mind is well familiar with the concept of "polarity" and the notion that apparent opposites can often be reconciled at some deeper level of understanding.[3]

It was, therefore, Schopenhauer's claim that intellect and matter

---

2. *WWR-2*, 15–16 (emphasis in original).
3. The philosophy sections of today's bookstores abound in popularizations of this viewpoint. Common examples in past years have been the works of Alan Watts, esp. Alan Watts, *The Way of Zen* (New York: Pantheon, 1958); *The Supreme Identity: An Essay on Oriental Metaphysic and the Christian Religion* (New York: Vintage Books, 1972); and *The Two Hands of God: The Myths of Polarity* (New York: Collier Books, 1963).

are one and the same thing, and can be seen as such at some transcendent, or deeper, level, namely, the level of the "will" or the "thing-in-itself"—the level of true reality unencumbered by time, space, causality, and the other impositions of the structure of the perceiving mind. Schopenhauer himself directed his readers to this Eastern mode of thought, quoting from Sir William Jones's *Asiatic Researches: On the Philosophy of the Asiatics*, vol. 4, p. 164:

> "The fundamental tenet of the Vedanta school consisted not in denying the existence of matter, that is, of solidity, impenetrability, and extended figure (to deny which would be lunacy), but in correcting the popular notion of it, and in contending that it has no essence independent of mental perception; that existence and perceptibility are convertible terms." These words adequately express the compatibility of empirical reality with transcendental ideality.[4]

Another step in Schopenhauer's filling of the gap between subject and object lies in his assertion that plurality (or, from a different vantage point, individuation) is, like time, space, and causality, an imposition of the structure of the perceiving mind and not an aspect of reality or "thing-in-itself." "Will" is one and undivided and, moreover, is fully present in each and in all of its objectified manifestations.

> [T]he *will* . . . is not one as an individual or a concept is, but as something to which the condition of the possibility of plurality, that is, the *principium individuationis,* is foreign. Therefore, the plurality of things in space and time that together are the *objectivity* of the will, does not concern the will, which, in spite of such plurality, remains indivisible. It is not a case of there being a smaller part of the will in the stone and a larger part in man,

4. *WWR*-1, 4.

for the relation of part and whole belongs exclusively to space, and has no longer any meaning the moment we have departed from this form of intuition or perception. . . . The will reveals itself just as completely and just as much in *one* oak as in millions.[5]

We will have occasion to revisit this doctrine of the presence of the will, whole and entire, in each of its manifestations, but as to the topic at hand—the subject/object relationship—if Schopenhauer is correct, then there is at the transcendent level no distinction between subject and object, just as there is no distinction between intellect and matter. They are both *will*. It is, perhaps, this insight of Schopenhauer's, that subject and object (or perceiving mind and world out there) are, at a transcendent level, one and the same thing, that shocks us so much. A contemporary quantum physicist would probably be less surprised. Physicist and author Fritjof Capra said it with some clarity:

> [T]he classical ideal of an objective description of nature is no longer valid. The Cartesian partition between the I and the world, between the observer and the observed, cannot be made when dealing with atomic matter. In atomic physics, we can never speak about nature without, at the same time, speaking about ourselves.[6]

This insight of Schopenhauer's concerning a basic identity at some deep level between perceiving subject and perceived object was not the only tenet of his (and Kant's) philosophy that contemporary physics has come around to accepting and, indeed, verifying in

---

5. *WWR*-1, 128 (emphasis in original).
6. Fritjof Capra, *The Tao of Physics*, 25th Anniversary ed. (Boston: Shambhala, 1999), 68–69 (hereinafter, Capra).

theory. Bryan Magee, perhaps somewhat tenuously, has seen Kant and Schopenhauer anticipating Einstein's famed principle of the equivalence of matter and energy:

> Perhaps the most astonishing of all the many Kantian-Schopenhauerian anticipations of modern science lies ... in the former's very specific announcement of one of the central doctrines of Einstein's theory of relativity more than a century before Einstein—the doctrine that (as Schopenhauer put it, following Kant): "force and substance are inseparable because at bottom they are one."[7]

Schopenhauer, of course, fit this principle of the equivalence of matter and energy into his theory of the "will" (the following few quotations are not easy reading):

> [S]ince matter is the visibility of the will, and every force in itself is will, no force can appear without a material sub-stratum, and conversely no body can exist without forces dwelling in it which constitute its quality. Thus a body is the union of matter and form which is called substance *(Stoff)*. *Force and substance are inseparable, because at bottom they are one;* for, as Kant has shown, matter itself is given to us only as the union of two forces, that of expansion and that of attraction. Therefore there exists no opposition between *force and substance;* on the contrary, they *are precisely one.*[8]

Matter is the "visibility" (manifestation?) of the will. "Force" is will in itself. A body is matter, that is, the "visibility" or manifestation of the will united with form. "Form" is also called "substance," and force and substance are one.

7. Magee, 112.
8. *WWR*-2, 309–10 (emphasis added).

Schopenhauer went on to explain the relationship between matter and force to some extent: "[T]he whole essence of matter consists in *acting;* only through this does it fill space and endure in time; it is through and through pure causality. Therefore wherever there is action there is matter, and the material is in general that which acts."[9] The essence of matter, that is, the visibility or manifestation of the will, is "acting" and is "pure causality." Recall that for Schopenhauer (as for Kant) the principle of causality is an imposition of the structure of the perceiving mind, and not an aspect of thing-in-itself, or reality out there. Also, for Schopenhauer, matter united with form, that is, substance *(Stoff),*[10] and force are not only "one"; they are the "will" itself: "[M]atter is the *will* itself [wrote Schopenhauer], yet no longer in itself, but in so far as it is *perceived,* that is to say, assumes the form of objective representation; thus what objectively is matter, subjectively is will."[11]

Elsewhere Schopenhauer called matter "that whereby the *will,* which constitutes the inner essence of things, enters into perceptibility, becomes perceptible or *visible.* Therefore in this sense matter is the mere visibility of the will, or the bond between the world as will and the world as representation."[12]

It is difficult to translate these difficult passages into the subatomic setting of the quantum physicist, but what Schopenhauer seems to be saying is that there is a basic ontological unity of organ of perception, thing perceived, and thing acting. To put it perhaps too simply, they are all "will." Matter is "will" perceived or observed — perceived or observed by "will" itself.

9. *WWR*-2, 305.
10. "Pure matter . . . constitutes the actual and legitimate content of the concept *substance.* . . ." *WWR*-2, 305.
11. *WWR*-2, 308 (emphasis in original).
12. *WWR*-2, 307 (emphasis in original).

Chapter 5

Platonic Ideas

The final link that Schopenhauer uses in filling the gap between subject and object is his understanding of the Platonic doctrine of Ideas. Schopenhauer's understanding is, however, somewhat different from what is popularly taken to be Plato's own meaning. Plato is popularly understood as holding that there is a separate world of Ideas, that that separate world is the "real" world, and that the world of our experience is only a flickering and indistinct reflection of it.[1] Schopenhauer scholar David W. Hamlyn explained "Schopenhauer is less concerned with the ontological status of the ideas than with their logical character as representations."[2] There is undoubted truth in Hamlyn's observation, but Schopenhauer would probably have responded that Plato too was less concerned with the ontological status of the Ideas than is commonly supposed. Plato's famed "Allegory of the Cave," Schopenhauer would have argued, is more prop-

---

1. Cf. Plato, *Republic*, bk. VII.
2. David W. Hamlyn, *Schopenhauer: The Arguments of the Philosophers* (London: Routledge, 1985), 104 (hereinafter, Hamlyn).

erly understood as an allegory of the sun, and bespeaks a form of enlightenment whereby the "thing-in-itself" of the subject can come to contemplate the "thing-in-itself" of the object from a unique and scarcely describable perspective—outside time itself. Plato put it this way:

> [T]he true analogy for this indwelling power in the soul and the instrument whereby each of us apprehends is that of an eye that could not be converted to the light from the darkness except by turning the whole body. Even so this organ of knowledge must be turned around from the world of *becoming* together with the entire soul, like the scene-shifting periactus in the theater, until the soul is able to endure the contemplation of the *essence* and the brightest region of *being*.[3]

We saw earlier that Schopenhauer found "will" to be the thing-in-itself of all reality by finding it first in the human subject's attempt to understand the true nature of the reality of his own self. In that context he found "will" to be directly and immediately presented (and not *re*presented) to the mind of the perceiving subject, and he reasoned that "will" or its non-self-conscious, or nonintelligent, or inanimate analogue is the thing-in-itself of all other reality. We cannot have direct, immediate knowledge of the thing-in-itself, the true reality, of objects outside ourselves, because our knowledge, since it is that of a perceiving subject, is conditioned by the structure of the instrument of perception, that is, our own mind. It is, according to Schopenhauer, the instrument of perception, or rather its structure or configuration, which imposes time, space, causality, and individuality on the objects of perception. We can only have direct, immedi-

---

3. Plato, *Republic*, bk. VII 518C, in *Plato: Collected Dialogues*, ed. Edith Hamilton and Huntington Cairns (New York: Pantheon Books, 1961), 750–51 (emphasis added).

ate knowledge of "will" in ourselves, because in that context, the context of our selves, we are both subject and object, or more properly perhaps, an entity in which subjectness and objectness are somehow fused.

The main problem with Schopenhauer's ontology is that even if one accepts his thesis that the perceiving subject can know "will" as the thing-in-itself of his own being, Schopenhauer gives us precious little justification for the conclusion that the perceiving subject can somehow understand that "will" is also the thing-in-itself of all *other* objects, or even that the perceiving subject can know anything at all about the thing-in-itself, the true reality, of other objects.

It is at this point that Schopenhauer's understanding of Plato's theory of Ideas comes to the rescue. Schopenhauer wrote, "Idea and thing-in-itself are *not* for us *absolutely* one and the same."[4] That is a cryptic and potentially misleading statement. The focus should be on the words "not . . . absolutely." There is obviously some strong connection between the Platonic Idea and the thing-in-itself, that is, true reality, and it is a connection that comes *close to* the two being "one and the same," but not *absolutely* so. For Schopenhauer, the Platonic Idea *is* the thing-in-itself, the true reality, but with one single limitation: it exists in the relationship that object bears to perceiving subject. That is its only limitation. It has none of the other limitations that ordinarily perceived items have; for example, it (the Platonic Idea) is timeless and spaceless.

The strong connection between the Platonic Idea and the thing-in-itself is made clear in Schopenhauer's treatment of aesthetics. Aesthetic concepts are difficult to verbalize. Schopenhauer wrote of "aesthetic pleasure" as encompassing

---

4. *WWR*-1, 174 (emphasis added).

the deliverance of knowledge from the service of the will, the forgetting of oneself as individual, and the enhancement of consciousness to the pure will-less, timeless subject of knowing that is independent of all relations. With this subjective side of aesthetic contemplation there always appears at the same time as necessary correlative its objective side, the intuitive apprehension of the Platonic Idea.[5]

To put it more simply, it is the Platonic Idea that the artist gleans from the scenery, and that the art appreciator gleans from the painting. It is the timeless and spaceless Platonic Idea that one finds in the object of one's love. It is an experiential glimpse of unindividuated oneness.

Schopenhauer's theory is both strong and weak at this point, that is, where he suggests a deep connection, falling just short of identity, between perceiving subject and perceived object at the level of the Platonic Idea. It is strong in that it seems to add to and to elucidate how it is that aesthetic appreciation exists and works. It is weak because it is not grounded in logical proof. This weakness, however, is perhaps tempered in modern scholarship in archetypal theory. There are connections between Schopenhauer's understanding of the Platonic Ideas and analytical psychologist Carl Jung's theory of archetypes and the collective unconscious. Jung, whose analytical psychology was deeply informed by Schopenhauerian thought, related his archetypes to Plato's Ideas and his concept of the collective unconscious to Schopenhauer's "will."[6]

Obviously, in Schopenhauer's thought, this contemplation of the Platonic Ideas is very much an occasional and exceptional activity. It

---

5. *WWR*-1, 199.
6. See, e.g., Carl G. Jung, *The Archetypes and the Collective Unconscious*, trans. R. F. C. Hull (Princeton, N.J.: Princeton University Press, 1969), 4, 277.

is not our normal way of perceiving—but it happens, and when it happens, the subject ceases "to be merely individual" and becomes "a pure will-less subject of knowledge" who has *im*mediate, that is, unmediated access to the "objectivity of the will." Schopenhauer explains it:

> [T]he transition that is possible, but to be regarded only as an exception, from the common knowledge of particular things to knowledge of the Idea takes place suddenly, since knowledge tears itself free from the service of the will precisely by the subject's ceasing to be merely individual, and being now a pure will-less subject of knowledge. . . . If therefore the object has to such an extent passed out of all relation to something outside it, and the subject has passed out of all relation to the will, what is thus known is no longer the individual thing as such, but the *Idea*, the eternal form, the immediate objectivity of the will at this grade.[7]

The subject-object distinction does not really disappear, but something does disappear in the experience—individuality. The perceiving subject is no longer divided from the perceived object by any mediating or re-presenting agency. In making this point, Schopenhauer quoted Byron for emphasis: "In this sense Byron says: 'Are not the mountains, waves and skies, a part of me and of my soul, as I of them.'"[8]

7. *WWR*-1, 178–79.
8. *WWR*-1, 181.

Chapter 6

Schopenhauer and Contemporary Scientific Theory

The first decade of the twentieth century encased a strange, shadow time. We seem to have named and placed clear associations on the decades that followed, for example, the Roaring Twenties, the Great Depression, and so on, but not on that first decade. On the surface, perhaps, it seemed to be a generally quiescent time, but underneath, political and social energies and forces were seething and stewing, largely unnoticed, and were soon to erupt in the Great War. In at least one context, however, that first decade of the twentieth century was far from quiescent, and in that context a dynamism was emerging that would justify referring to the decade as an era of stunning creativity and achievement.

Physicist Max Planck inaugurated the twentieth century by bringing forth the first crucial idea of what was eventually to become the theory of quantum mechanics:[1] the notion that energy exists in

---

1. See Heinz R. Pagels, *The Cosmic Code: Quantum Physics As the Language of Nature* (New York: Bantam Books, 1982), 11 (hereinafter, Pagels).

the form of discrete quantities and that the emission and absorption of energy occurs in packets, or bunches, or "quanta." In 1905 Albert Einstein published three papers and wrote a fourth. His first paper proposed what is now recognized as the first convincing test for demonstrating the existence of atoms.[2] The second posited that light—light had been thought of up to that time as wave rather than particle—as well as matter was "quantized," that is, existed in the form of a rain of discrete particles which we now refer to as photons.[3] The third introduced his special theory of relativity, which linked space and time as two aspects of one and the same phenomenon.[4] Einstein's fourth paper, written in 1905 and further developed in 1907, showed the equivalence of matter and energy in the now well known formula $e = mc^2$.[5] Planck's modest beginnings in reinterpreting Newtonian mechanics and Einstein's stunning insights were to alter forever not only the principles of physics as then understood and accepted, but (as we are now coming to realize) our basic understanding of reality itself.

This modern Scientific Re-enlightenment finds its contemporary expression in two sets of theories: Einstein's theories of relativity and the theories of quantum mechanics developed by Neils Bohr, Werner Heisenberg, and others. Relativity theory speaks to understandings of reality at the macro level, if you will, the cosmic level of galactic space. Quantum theory, on the other hand, speaks to understandings of reality on the micro level, the level of subatomic events. It is in the implications of the theory of quantum mechanics that Schopenhauer's metaphysics find their closest analogue.

Two seemingly different and opposed approaches within quantum mechanics have received considerable attention, Werner Heisenberg's uncertainty principle and Neils Bohr's principle of complementarity. According to the uncertainty principle, it is impossible to

2. Pagels, 14. 3. Pagels, 15.
4. Pagels, 18. 5. Pagels, 21.

measure the position and the momentum of a subatomic particle (such as an electron) at the same time. Granting "reality" to the one destroys it for the other. According to the principle of complementarity, "particle" and "wave" are concepts that exclude one another, and yet certain subatomic entities can be correctly represented as a particle *and* as a wave, although not at the same time. Bohr's and Heisenberg's principles, taken together, have come to be known as the "Copenhagen Interpretation" of quantum mechanics and, taken together, they have an unsettling implication.

Objectivity, in quantum theory, seems to be something that we, the "observers," fix on reality, something that we grant to the world out there, at least to the world at the subatomic level. In the words of physicist Heinz Pagels, "The Copenhagen Interpretation of the new quantum theory ended the classical idea of objectivity—the idea that the world has a definite state of existence independent of our observing it."[6]

One, of course, thinks immediately of Immanuel Kant's tenet that the structure of the perceiving mind affects the perception of reality and of his cryptic formulation: "[I]t is clearly shown that if I remove the thinking subject the whole corporeal world must at once vanish."[7] It is not without significance that the scientific theories of today seem to support the basic premise inherent in Kant's "Copernican Revolution." There is an ontological interconnectedness between the subjective and the objective, and from the subjective vantage point, time, space, causality, and even individuality itself are conceptions that we, to some extent at least, fix on reality; they are not properties of objects-in-themselves. Astrophysicist and science writer John Gribben expressed the subatomic oddities inherent in the "Copenhagen Interpretation," using the electron as an example:

6. Pagels, 114.
7. Kant, *Pure Reason*, 354.

In the Copenhagen Interpretation, an entity such as an electron is neither a wave nor a particle, but something different, something we cannot describe in everyday language. But it will show us either a particle face or a wave face, depending on which measurements we choose to carry out on it. . . .[8]

Gribben's assessment of the Copenhagen Interpretation brings us to Erwin Schrödinger's cat-in-the-box thought experiment. The experiment illustrates nicely the "something" that "we cannot describe in everyday language" and gives us an inkling of *why* we cannot describe it in everyday language. Schrödinger used an atomic-decay apparatus and a cat inside a box in his original 1935 formulation of the thought experiment,[9] but Gribben later reformulated the scenario:

[I]magine a box [wrote Gribben] which contains a single electron. If nobody looks in the box, then according to the Copenhagen Interpretation there is an equal probability of finding the electron anywhere inside the box—the probability wave associated with the electron fills the box uniformly. Now imagine that, still without anyone looking inside the box, a partition is automatically lowered in the middle of the box, dividing it into two equal boxes. Common sense tells us that the electron must be in

---

8. Gribben, *Kittens*, 16.
9. Schrödinger, in his original 1935 formulation of the thought experiment, hypothesized the radioactive decay of an atom: "A cat is penned up in a steel chamber, along with the following diabolical device (which must be secured against direct interference by the cat): in a Geiger counter there is a tiny bit of radioactive substance, so small, that perhaps in the course of one hour one of the atoms decays, but also with equal probability, perhaps none; if it happens, the counter tube discharges and through a relay releases a hammer which shatters a small flask of hydrocyanic acid. If one has left this entire system to itself for an hour, one would say that the cat lives if meanwhile no atom has decayed. The first atomic decay would have poisoned it." Quoted in P. C. W. Davies and J. R. Brown, *The Ghost in the Atom* (Cambridge: Cambridge University Press, 1986), 29.

one side of the box or the other. But the Copenhagen Interpretation tells us that the probability wave [of the electron] is still evenly distributed across both half-boxes. . . . The wave only collapses, with the electron becoming "real," when somebody looks into the boxes and notices [on] which side of the partition the electron is. At that moment, the probability wave on the other side of the partition vanishes.[10]

That is the setting for the thought experiment. Schrödinger suggested the placing of a cat inside the box itself, but Gribben, in an apparent effort to blunt the more "hellish" implications of having the cat in the small box, has the cat in his updated version in a closed, windowless room, along with the box on a table in the room. Then the experiment is conducted (but only in thought, thankfully). The one lone electron is inserted into the box and the partition is automatically lowered, dividing the box into two equal halves. In Gribben's version, there is an electron-detecting device that is wired to an apparatus that will flood the room with poison gas if it detects an electron outside the box. One half of the box is then opened. If the electron had been in that half, it is now in the open room and the poison gas is released, killing the cat. If the electron had been in the unopened half of the box, then it has not been detected, and the cat is still alive. Gribben's conclusion is that, under the Copenhagen Interpretation:

> [T]he wave function of the whole system does not collapse until a *conscious* observer (preferably equipped with a gas mask, if they want to be sure of staying conscious) opens the door to look inside. At that moment, and *only* at that moment, the electron "decides" whether it is inside or outside the box, the detec-

---

10. Gribben, *Kittens*, 19.

tor "decides" whether it has found the electron or not, and the cat "decides" whether it is dead or alive. Until somebody looks inside the room, the Copenhagen Interpretation describes the situation as a "superposition of states"—or, in Schrödinger's words, having in it the living and the dead cat (pardon the expression) mixed or smeared out in equal parts.[11]

During the interim between the opening of the one-half of the box, and the point at which a conscious observer enters the room, *the cat*, according to the Copenhagen Interpretation, *is both alive and dead.*

11. Gribben, *Kittens*, 21 (emphasis added).

Chapter 7

Ontological "Oneness"

In 1975, theoretical physicist Fritjof Capra published a popularization of quantum theory under the title *The Tao of Physics*. The book also carried a subtitle: *An Exploration of the Parallels Between Modern Physics and Eastern Mysticism*. Capra's book became a best seller, went into second and third editions, and has had a profound effect—it has opened to the general public the quandary we have been discussing, the fact that contemporary quantum theory has radically altered our Western scientific understandings of space, time, matter, causality, and objectivity. In Capra's words,

> [a]t the subatomic level, matter does not exist with certainty at definite places, but rather shows "tendencies to exist," and atomic events do not occur with certainty at definite times and in definite ways, but rather show "tendencies to occur." . . . At the subatomic level, the solid material objects of classical physics dissolve into wavelike patterns of probabilities, and these patterns, ultimately, do not represent probabilities of things, but

rather probabilities of interconnections.... Quantum theory thus reveals the basic oneness of the universe.[1]

Schopenhauer had no less difficulty than Capra in articulating the point:

> There yet remains something on which no explanation can venture, but which it presupposes, namely the forces of nature, the definite mode of operation of things, the quality, the character of every phenomenon, the groundless, that which depends not on the form of the phenomenon, not on the principle of sufficient reason, that to which this form in itself is foreign, yet which has entered this form, and now appears according to its law. This law, however, determines only the appearing, not *that which* appears, only the *how*, not the *what* of the phenomenon, only its form, not its content.
>
> ...
>
> [I]n everything in nature there is something to which no ground can ever be assigned, for which no explanation is possible, and no further cause is to be sought.... [T]his, I say, is to the mote what man's *will* is to man; and, like the human will, it is in its inner nature not subject to explanation.[2]

Tendencies to exist ... tendencies to occur ... patterns ... probabilities of interconnections. Reaching for a word that is not quite there. Schopenhauer chose the word "will."

Schopenhauer's dual world is a strange one indeed—every bit as strange as the dual world of the quantum theorists. At the ordinary level—the phenomenal level, that is, the level at which we normally perceive things—we experience things and events as discrete and

1. Capra, 68.
2. *WWR*-1, 121, 122, 124.

concrete "realities." But at that other level, the level of true reality, the level of thing-in-itself—the noumenal level—it is quite a different situation. At that deep level, which we can experience only dimly and inferentially, all is "will," a chaos of tendency—a tendency to exist, to live, and to survive.

What we have learned in recent years, with the now well-accepted principles that flow from the special and general theories of relativity and the theory of quantum physics, is that we do indeed live in a dual world: the world of ordinary perception in which we experience things and events as discrete and concrete "realities," and another world, a world in which time and space are one, in which the concept of causality is jettisoned along with the concept of simultaneity, and in which the "building blocks" of matter are nothing but tendencies and potentialities. Physicist Nick Herbert has summarized the situation:

> According to Heisenberg [wrote Herbert], there is no deep reality—nothing down there that's real in the same sense as the phenomenal facts are real. . . . [T]he atoms and the elementary particles . . . form a world of potentialities or possibilities rather than one of things or facets. . . . The probability wave . . . means a tendency for something. . . . It introduces something standing in the middle between the idea of an event and the actual event, a strange kind of physical reality just in the middle between possibility and reality.
> . . .
> The quantum world . . . is not a world of actual events like our own but a world full of numerous unrealized tendencies for action. These tendencies are continually on the move, growing, merging, and dying. . . .
> . . .

Ontological "Oneness" 47

> Everything that happens in our world arises out of possibilities prepared for in that other—the world of quantum potentia. . . . *There is no deep reality, no deep reality-as-we-know-it.* Instead the unobserved universe consists of *possibilities, tendencies, urges.*[3]

What classical physics tells us is that the world of our experience is a world of spatially and temporally located interacting particles of matter. But that is not the whole story. It may be the world of our experience, but it is not the world of true, deep down reality. It is not the world that contemporary quantum physics sees. Deep down, below the submicroscopic level if you will, the world is not a world of spatially and temporally located particles of matter. "Particleness" itself—even particularity itself—is a subjective imposition that enters the picture only when an "observer" enters the fray. Unobserved, true reality, at its deepest level, consists of "possibilities, tendencies, urges." Even at that submicroscopic level, it seems difficult to avoid anthropomorphisms, like "urges." If one were to indulge in further anthropomorphic description, and perhaps raise the description to the level of human psychology itself, it does not seem too far off the mark to equate possibilities, tendencies, and urges with opportunities, affections, and motivations. The quantum physicists may indeed be telling us that the world, at that level of deep reality, *is* "will" (or its dehumanized, inanimate correspondent), and that what we take to be the attributes of "matter" are really subjective impositions, that is, events that occur in the acts of observing and perceiving. It seems difficult to conclude otherwise, or so one might imagine Schopenhauer arguing.

The quantum physicist is on much the same quest as the meta-

---

3. Nick Herbert, *Quantum Reality: Beyond the New Physics* (Garden City, N.Y.: Anchor Books, 1987), 26–27 (emphasis added) (hereinafter, Herbert).

physician. Both seek to understand the ultimate nature of reality. We saw earlier that Schopenhauer and the contemporary quantum physicists have reached remarkably similar conclusions as to the subjectivity of space and time and even as to the ultimate moving force behind, or the grounding of, reality itself. The physicists speak of tendencies, urges, and probabilities. Schopenhauer speaks of "will" in a broad, analogical sense. One might wonder whether the quantum physicists are reaching a similar conclusion on the problem of the unity or plurality of the universe.

One dilemma exposed by the quantum physicists dealing with the nature of matter at the subatomic level is that if the world is made out of separate entities, then what is now known about subatomic particle interaction requires that some of these subatomic entities have the power to move faster than the speed of light.[4] According to Einstein's special theory of relativity, the speed of light is, ontologically, the universal speed limit. Einstein demonstrated that as an object approaches the speed of light, its mass increases to the point where, at the speed of light, it has infinite mass. An infinite mass would, of course, require an infinite amount of energy to move it.[5] This anomaly and other findings in the area of quantum mechanics have led many physicists to the conclusion that there is indeed a basic oneness to the universe.

Albert Einstein and two other physicists, Boris Podolsky and Nathan Rosen, first highlighted the dilemma. Einstein was never quite satisfied with the uncertainty posited by quantum theory. His famous statement "I cannot believe that God plays dice with the universe"[6] is an articulation of that dissatisfaction. Nor was he satisfied

4. See, e.g., Herbert, 28.
5. See Albert Einstein, *Relativity: The Special and the General Theory* (New York: Crown Publishers, 1961), 35–37.
6. Quoted in Herbert, 199.

with the implications within quantum theory to the effect that reality is, at least in part, "observer-created."[7] In 1935, the same year in which Erwin Schrödinger posited his cat-in-the-box thought experiment, Einstein, Podolsky, and Rosen posited a thought experiment of their own in order to demonstrate the impossibility of those uncertainty and observer-creation implications of quantum theory. The experiment has come to be known as the EPR (Einstein-Podolsky-Rosen) experiment or EPR paradox. It is explained in most if not all of the popular treatises on quantum theory.[8]

Very roughly, the EPR paradox builds on the quantum principle that once two subatomic entities are connected with each other (Einstein, Podolsky, and Rosen used protons, but other formulations of the experiment have used two photons), and then are made to separate, they remain mysteriously connected in some way. If the subatomic polarization characteristic of one of the entities is, say, "up," the subatomic polarization characteristic of the other has to be the opposite, say, "down." Quantum physicists describe the very esoteric characteristics of subatomic entities by prosaic names, such as, for example, "up" or "down" or even in terms of the names of assorted "colors." Recall now that, in quantum theory, reality is at least in part "observer-created." The characteristic, for example, up or down, is merely a *potentiality* until an observer, to use the phraseology of the quantum physicists, "collapses the wave function" by observing it (the entity now appearing as a particle rather than as a wave). It is at that moment, *and not before,* that the "up-ness" or "down-ness" of the subatomic entity becomes fixed. Now, quantum theory also demands that the same characteristic in the subatomic entity to which the observed entity was once connected be also fixed, *instantaneously*. It does not matter whether the now unconnected subatomic entity

7. Herbert, 199.
8. See, e.g., Gribben, *Kittens*, 23–28.

is a mile away or at the other end of the universe. The fixing of the characteristic is *instantaneous,* wherever it is. To Einstein, Podolsky, and Rosen, this meant that the fact of the observation, that is, the fact of the collapsing of the wave function, would have to be communicated to the now-unconnected subatomic entity faster than is possible. Instantaneous communication is an impossibility according to Einstein's special theory of relativity. The speed of light (approximately 300,000 km/sec.)[9] is the universal speed limit.

Einstein, Podolsky, and Rosen believed that their thought experiment could never be tested, but Irish physicist John Bell in the 1960s found a way of testing the matter, at least in principle, in a theorem he posed. In the 1980s, French physicist Alain Aspect and his colleagues actually carried out the testing. The result, to make a long story short, is that the kind of instantaneous communication at a distance demanded by quantum theory does indeed occur. This has led to the utterly counter-intuitive yet necessarily valid conclusion that, at the subatomic level where quantum theory operates, the universe is *nonlocal:*

> The results of experiments testing Bell's theorem clearly reveal that Einstein's assumption in the EPR thought experiment—that correlations between paired protons over space-like separated regions could not possibly occur—was wrong. The experiments show that the correlations do, in fact, hold over any distance instantly, or in "no time." Since this violates assumptions in local realistic theories, physical reality is not, as Einstein felt it should and must be, local. The experiments clearly indicate that physical reality is non-local.[10]

---

9. Actually, 299,742.458 in a vacuum.
10. Robert Nadeau and Menas Kafatos, *The Non-Local Universe: The New Physics and Matters of the Mind* (Oxford: Oxford University Press, 1999), 74.

Ontological "Oneness"　51

At the deep down level of true reality all is one interconnected whole. Schopenhauer had argued that at the deep down level of true reality, plurality or individuation does not exist. Separateness, plurality, individuation are merely subjective impositions of the perceiving mind and not an aspect of true reality, the "thing-in-itself."

Physicist Fritjof Capra put it thus:

> A careful analysis of the process of observation in atomic physics has shown that the subatomic particles have no meaning as isolated entities, but can only be understood as interconnections between the preparation of an experiment and the subsequent measurement. *Quantum theory thus reveals a basic oneness of the universe. It shows that we cannot decompose the world into independently existing smallest units.* As we penetrate into matter, nature does not show us any isolated "basic building blocks," but rather appears as a complicated web of relations between various parts of the whole.[11]

Recall Schopenhauer's insight that the "will" is one and undivided and, moreover, is fully present, whole and entire, in each and in all of its objectified manifestations.

> [T]he *will* . . . is not one as an individual or a concept is, but as something to which the condition of the possibility of plurality, that is, the *principium individuationis,* is foreign. Therefore, the plurality of things in space and time that together are the *objectivity* of the will, does not concern the will, which, in spite of such plurality, remains indivisible. It is not a case of there being a smaller part of the will in the stone and a larger part in man, for the relation of part and whole belongs exclusively to space,

---

11. Capra, 68 (emphasis added); see also 130–43.

and has no longer any meaning the moment we have departed from this form of intuition or perception. . . . The will reveals itself just as completely and just as much in *one* oak as in millions.[12]

If, as both Schopenhauer and the quantum physicists suggest, there is an interconnectedness, a "basic oneness," to the universe, why do we seem to observe plurality and individuation? To Schopenhauer, of course, plurality and individuation belong only to the world at the level of phenomena, not to the true, underlying reality of the world as "will." Quantum physicist David Bohm has a similar explanation: "Fragmentation is continually being brought about by the almost universal habit of taking the content of our thought for a 'description of the world as it is.' . . . [W]holeness is what is real."[13]

As is not uncommon among quantum physicists who write for the lay public (Erwin Schrödinger being perhaps the lone exception), Bohm cites Kant far more frequently than he cites Schopenhauer to explain what he means by fragmentation being illusory: "As seems to have been first pointed out by Kant, all experience is organized according to the categories of our thought, i.e., on our ways of thinking about space, time, matter, substance, causality, contingency, necessity, universality, particularity, etc."[14]

Schopenhauer was, as we have seen, in total agreement with this thesis of Kant, that is, that we perceive things as adhering to the principle of cause and effect, and as existing in time and space, *not* because the things-in-themselves actually *do* adhere to the principle of cause and effect and actually *do* exist in time and space, but rather because the very structure of the perceiving mind imposes causality,

---

12. *WWR*-1, 128 (emphasis in original).
13. David Bohm, *Wholeness and the Implicate Order* (London: Routledge, 1980), 3, 7 (hereinafter, Bohm).
14. Bohm, 5–6.

time, and space on our perceptions of the things, and made this thesis the touchstone of his entire philosophy.

And so we seem to have come full circle. The quantum physicists are becoming metaphysicians, perhaps even Schopenhauerian metaphysicians. But there is more. Max Planck, the progenitor of quantum mechanics, once wrote: "Science . . . means unresting endeavor and continually progressing development toward an aim which the poetic intuition may apprehend, but which the intellect can never fully grasp."[15] We all recognize the euphonious chord struck by John Donne's "No Man is an Island," and it is likely that Donne's was one of the poetic sensibilities Planck had in mind as he saw the implications of quantum mechanics moving toward the notion that everything in the universe is really an interconnected wholeness. Most of us would probably recognize another euphonious chord in another poetic epithet, this one by William Blake:

> To see a world in a grain of sand
> And a heaven in a wild flower,
> Hold infinity in the palm of your hand
> And Eternity in an hour.[16]

Many quantum theorists seem unable to avoid a line of thought developing towards recognition of that poetic sensibility, that is, that the entire universe is contained in any and every particle. It is, perhaps, not surprising that some quantum theorists have been led in that direction. For example, quantum physicist David Bohm's "multi-dimensional implicate-order" interpretation of quantum theory allows some measure of truth to Blake's poetic sensibility. Fritjof Capra

---

15. Max Planck, *The Philosophy of Physics*, trans. W. H. Johnston (New York: W. W. Norton, 1936), 83; also quoted in Gary Zukav, *The Dancing Wu Li Masters: An Overview of the New Physics* (New York: Perennial Classics, 2001), 347.

16. William Blake, "Auguries of Innocence," reprinted in *The Portable Blake*, ed. A. Kazin (Middlesex: Penguin Books, 1974), 150.

sees that sensibility as a logical tenet of Bohm's and others' interpretations of quantum theory:

> [T]he universe is an interconnected whole in which no part is any more fundamental than the other, so that the properties of any one part are determined by those of all the others. In that sense, one might say that every part "contains" all the others and, indeed, a vision of mutual embodiment seems to be characteristic of the mystical experience in nature.[17]

Bohm devised a thought model of his own in an effort to illustrate his understanding of the implications of the Einstein-Podolsky-Rosen paradox and the faster-than-light communication and nonlocality that the paradox demands. Bohm's thought model did not involve a cat, as did Schopenhauer's and Schrödinger's. Instead it involved a fish:

> Let us begin [wrote Bohm] with a rectangular tank full of water, with transparent walls [an ordinary household fish tank, in other words]. Suppose further that there are two television cameras . . . directed at what is going on in the water (e.g., fish swimming around) as seen through the two walls *at right angles* to each other. Now let the corresponding television images be made available on [two different television] screens . . . in another room. What we will see there is a certain *relationship* between the images appearing on the two screens. At any given moment each image will generally *look* different from the other. Nevertheless the differences will be related, in the sense that when one image is seen to execute certain movements, the other will be seen to execute corresponding movements.[18]

17. Capra, 292.
18. Bohm, 187.

It is just an analogy, of course, but Bohm's point is well understood. A three-dimensional object (the fish) seen two-dimensionally (i.e., on the surfaces of two different television screens) from two different angles will appear to be two different objects, but with their characteristics and movements in precise and *instantaneous* synchronization. Yet we know, because we have the "Big Picture," that it is really only one object viewed from two different angles, and the precise and instantaneous synchronization is just a chimera. The "two" fish exist only in our imagination. Bohm's point is that in the context of the EPR paradox, what appears to the quantum physicist observers as two different subatomic entities separated three-dimensionally yet behaving precisely and instantaneously in unison, is really, if it could be viewed *multi*-dimensionally, one and the same subatomic entity.

> What we are proposing here [wrote Bohm] is that the quantum property of a nonlocal, noncausal relationship of distant elements may be understood through an extension of the notion described above [i.e., the "fish" thought illustration]. That is to say, we may regard each of the "particles" constituting the system as a projection of a "higher-dimensional" reality, rather than as a separate particle, existing together with all the others in a common three-dimensional space.[19]

The universe (and everything in it) is indeed nonlocal, Bohm agrees, but faster-than-light communication between subatomic entities is not required.

Bohm also had something to offer in the context of (but without mentioning) Schopenhauer's insight that the "will" is one and undivided and, moreover, is *fully* present, whole and entire, in each and

---

19. Bohm, 188.

in all of its objectified manifestations. How can *all* of deep down reality-in-itself be present in each phenomenal manifestation, that is, in each apparently separate entity? In Schopenhauerian terms, how can the "will" be fully present, *whole and entire,* in each of its objectified manifestations? Bohm's answer was to draw the concept of the *hologram* into the picture:

> [R]elativity and quantum theory [wrote Bohm] imply undivided wholeness, in which analysis into distinct and well-defined parts is no longer relevant. Is there an instrument that can help give a certain immediate perceptual insight into what can be meant by undivided wholeness . . . ? It is suggested here that one can obtain such insight by considering *hologram.*[20]

Bohm's use of the hologram is, of course, like his use of the fish, merely an analogy.[21] Just as each part of a hologram contains the whole picture, enfolded, as it were, so too each "part" of reality contains the whole of reality, "implicate" or enfolded. Bohm's main thesis is contained in the title of his book intended for the lay public, *Wholeness and the Implicate Order,* in much the same way as Schopenhauer's main thesis is contained in the title of his masterwork, *The World as Will and Representation.* Bohm explained "wholeness" and the "implicate order":

> We proposed that a new motion of order is involved here, which we call the *implicate order* (from a Latin root meaning "to enfold" or "to fold inward"). In terms of the implicate order one may say that everything is enfolded into everything. This contrasts with the *explicate order* now dominant in physics in which

---

20. Bohm, 144–45 (emphasis in original).
21. The utility of the hologram analogy and its implications are explored extensively in Michael Talbot, *The Holographic Universe* (New York: Harper Perennial, 1991).

things are *unfolded* in the sense that each thing lies only in its own particular region of space (and time) and outside the regions belonging to other things.[22]

Here we see what is perhaps the most radical of Schopenhauer's theses seemingly confirmed in a major interpretation of quantum theory. The whole "will"—in quantum terms, the whole of reality—is contained in each of its apparently separate manifestations.

Later, we shall have occasion to look into Schopenhauer's connections with Quietist mystical theology. One mystical theologian, whose writings were never cited by Schopenhauer, but apparently were well known to David Bohm,[23] was Nicholas of Cusa, a fifteenth-century Cardinal of the Catholic Church. The following passage illustrates the remarkable resonance among the quantum thoughts of David Bohm, the thesis of Schopenhauer, and the fifteenth-century mystical insights of Nicholas of Cusa:

> [In] Cusa's philosophy, . . . each individual being relates to all being in that each is a contraction *(contractio)* of the whole. In *De Docta Ignorantia* ["On Learned Ignorance," Cusa's magnum opus], Cusa defines the term contraction as the restriction of Being itself to some particular thing.
>
> Thus the whole Being exists in a restricted fashion in each particular being. In this sense, each existing creature, reflects not merely every other creature, but also the entirety of being.[24]

---

22. Bohm, 177 (emphasis in original).
23. See P. C. W. Davies and J. R. Brown, *The Ghost in the Atom* (Cambridge: Cambridge University Press, 1999), 122.
24. David J. De Leonardis, *Ethical Implications of Unity and the Divine in Nicholas of Cusa* (Washington, D.C.: The Council for Research in Values and Philosophy, 1998), 44.

Schrödinger's Metaphysical Ethical Insight

We have seen that pioneer quantum physicist Erwin Schrödinger was quite familiar with the writings of Schopenhauer.[25] At one point in his philosophical treatise, Schrödinger quoted and commented at length on a bit of poetry from Schopenhauer's writings, expressing a sentiment that Schopenhauer said "was his comfort in life and would be his comfort in death."[26]

> The one all-highest Godhead
> Subsisting in each being
> And living when they perish—
> Who this has seen, is seeing.
> For he who has that highest God in all things found,
> That man will of himself upon himself inflict no wound.[27]

Tracing the poem to the Hindu Scriptures, Schrödinger criticized the Brahman doctrine of reincarnation and the transmigration of souls [28] on which the sentiments of the poem seemed to be based (criticizing as well the Hindu caste system), but he praised the words of the poem as "beautiful" and the ethic that underlay them as "lovely"[29] and quite agreeable:

---

25. Schrödinger, viii.
26. Schrödinger, 104 (written by Schrödinger in 1960).
27. Schrödinger, 96 (written by Schrödinger in 1960). A bit of interpretive translation may seem to be in order here. Schopenhauer, who regarded these apparently theistic verses as his "comfort" in life and death, certainly was no theist. The "Godhead" or "God" in the verses cannot be the Personal God of traditional theism. The "Godhead" or "God" (to Schopenhauer) must be the impersonal will posited by Schopenhauer as subsisting in all things. To Schopenhauer, the verses must mean that one who has seen and found this "Godhead" or "God" (i.e., the will) in all things will see through or transcend the world of phenomena, where the will constantly wounds itself, and will no longer participate in that self-wounding.
28. Schrödinger, 102–3 (written by Schrödinger in 1960).
29. Schrödinger, 104 (written by Schrödinger in 1960).

Ontological "Oneness" 59

> Mercy and kindness towards all living beings (not only our fellow-men) are here [i.e., in the quoted poem] praised as the highest attainable goal—in very much the same sense as Albert Schweitzer's "reverence for life." . . . So much for the ethical conclusion drawn by Indian philosophy from the (unprovable) thesis that we living beings are all simply sides or aspects of one single Being; a conclusion with which . . . I, with Albert Schweitzer, am very willing to agree.[30]

After discussing a morality based on rules and proverbs, Schrödinger had this to say: "But there seems to us to be more nobility in that other view . . . which that poor pessimist Arthur Schopenhauer described as his comfort in life and in death. It is quite irrelevant whether Schopenhauer himself lived in accordance with this higher ethic."[31]

Schrödinger, in pure Schopenhauerian rhetoric, identified "that other view" with "the basic Vedantic vision"[32] and in the process quoted one of Schopenhauer's mentors, the immortal Goethe: "And thy spirit's highest fiery flight / Is satisfied with likeness and with image."[33] Perhaps most startling in Schrödinger's treatment of "the Vedantic vision" was his acceptance of the concept of ontological oneness that is being discovered and accepted today by quantum physicists and metaphysicians:

> [I]nconceivable as it seems to ordinary reason [wrote Schrödinger], you—and all other conscious beings as such—are all in all. Hence this life of yours which you are living is not merely a piece of the entire existence, but is in a certain sense

30. Schrödinger, 97–98 (written by Schrödinger in 1960).
31. Schrödinger, 109 (written by Schrödinger in 1960).
32. Schrödinger, 18, 19 (written by Schrödinger in 1925).
33. Schrödinger, 18 (written by Schrödinger in 1925).

the *whole;* only this whole is not so constituted that it can be surveyed in one single glance.[34]

In what "certain sense" is this life of each of us the *whole* of existence? Schrödinger explained:

> This . . . is what the Brahmins express in that sacred, mystic formula which is yet so simple and so clear: *Tat tvam asi,* this is you. Or again in such words as 'I am in the east and in the west, I am below and above, I am this whole world.' [And] It is the vision of this truth . . . which underlies all morally valuable activity.[35]

In a chapter headed "More About Non-Plurality," Schrödinger developed the Vedantic theme of ontological oneness further:

> To divide or multiply consciousness is something meaningless. . . . [C]onsciousness in the plural . . . is simply something we construct because of the spatio-temporal plurality of individuals, but it is a false construction. Because of it all philosophy succumbs again and again to the hopeless conflict between the theoretically unavoidable acceptance of Berkeleian idealism and its complete uselessness for understanding the real world. [Recall from Chapter 3 supra Schopenhauer's criticism of the Kantian ethic as based in pure subjective idealism.] The only solution to this conflict, in so far as any is available to us at all, lies in the ancient wisdom of the Unpanishads.[36]

Schrödinger, in the perhaps overly modest conclusion to his treatment of ethics informed by the discoveries of quantum physics, gave

---

34. Schrödinger, 21, 22 (written by Schrödinger in 1925).
35. Schrödinger, 22 (written by Schrödinger in 1925).
36. Schrödinger, 31 (written by Schrödinger in 1925).

total credit to Schopenhauer: "I was not [wrote Schrödinger] trying here to show forth the motives of ethical action, to exhibit a new 'foundation for morality.' Schopenhauer, we know, did that, and it is scarcely likely that in this direction there will be anything essential as yet to add to what he said."[37]

It is important to note that although Erwin Schrödinger wrote much of the above at an early stage in his career, he published it long after he had worked out the wave equation that bears his name and on which quantum mechanics is based.[38] Schrödinger published his metaphysical treatise in 1961. He had worked out the Schrödinger wave equation in 1926 and received his Nobel Prize in 1933. One may surmise that, as with Schopenhauer whose youthful insights never changed, these were youthful insights that became, over the years, the mature insights of one of the founders of quantum mechanics, developed over and ensconced firmly and comfortably in a lifetime of work in quantum theory.

37. Schrödinger, 58 (written by Schrödinger in 1925).
38. See, e.g., Brian Greene, *The Fabric of the Cosmos: Space, Time, and the Texture of Reality* (New York: Alfred A. Knopf, 2004), 200; and Michio Kaku and Jennifer Thompson, *Beyond Einstein: The Cosmic Quest for the Theory of the Universe* (New York: Anchor Books, 1995), 39.

Chapter 8

Justice and the
Principium Individuationis

Schopenhauer's theory of justice can thus be seen as being quite consistent with both David Bohm's "multi-dimensional implicate-order" interpretation of quantum theory and William Blake's poetic sensibility, and as leading inexorably to the ethic that Erwin Schrödinger discussed. Indeed Bohm's interpretation, Blake's sensibility, and the ethic seen by Schrödinger all seem to flow naturally from Schopenhauer's understanding of "will" as "thing in itself." "Will," in Schopenhauer's thought, is "the sole kernel of every phenomenon." It "reveals itself just as completely and just as much in *one* oak as in millions."[1] It lies outside time, space, causality, and individuation. It is one. For Schopenhauer, it is also without consciousness, and groundless in itself. It is itself the essence, the thing-in-itself, of all individuated phenomena or things. Because "will" is unindividuated, it is present, unindividuated, whole and entire (in

1. *WWR*-1, 118, 128.

Bohmian terms, the whole of reality is "implicate" or enfolded), in each apparently separate phenomenon or thing. The "will" is one, but it can only manifest itself in the plurality of individuals. That is, according to Schopenhauer, it can only manifest itself *to the human mind* in the plurality of individual things. This is because human knowledge can only exist in the forms dictated by the structure of human intelligence, that is, time, space, causality, individuation, et cetera.

With the human mind, the "will" becomes, to some extent, conscious—but "conscious" only in a limited and imperfect way. Through the human mind, the "will" "perceives around it the innumerably repeated image of its own inner being."[2] But it is present, whole and entire, in every objectification of itself; that is to say, plurality is an illusion. And so every individual, that is, every *knowing* individual, finds himself as the *whole* "will," simply because at the deep level of reality he in truth *is* the whole "will."

The "will" *is* being-in-itself. In most of the phenomenal world, the "will" expresses itself as a will to *exist*. For example, the ground of being of rocks and stars is, simply put, the tendency to exist, or, as the quantum physicists might put it, the patterns of probability of interaction that lead to their existence as "real" entities. But there seems to be a progression or gradation of being. Some parts of the world of phenomena have what seems to us to be a higher type of being, that is, *living* being. In living being, the "will" becomes, to a lesser or greater extent, conscious of itself as a tendency, and to that lesser or greater extent (depending on the level of sophistication of the life form) becomes what the human being would readily recognize as "will," and thus expresses itself as a will to *live*. Since the "will" knows no individuation, it "cares" only for existence and life as such, and not for any particularized manifestations of existence or

2. *WWR*-1, 352.

life. Indeed, at the deep level of true reality, there are no particular manifestations of existence or life; individuation and plurality exist only at the phenomenal level. According to Schopenhauer, plurality is an illusion, a form of knowledge imposed by the structure of the human mind. Consequently, at the plant and lower animal level, "will" seems to be at war with itself. Existence and life as such are enhanced, but at the cost of what appears to us as the destruction of the weaker individual manifestations of the will to live by the stronger. But on its own level, the level of true reality, this warring or "destruction" is simply the aimless striving for being or living that *is* the "will."

Enter now the higher forms of animal life, culminating in human life, with consciousness and the capacity for cognition and ultimately for self-reflection, and the "will" comes to have a limited form of knowledge of itself. With these higher forms of animal life, "the mirror of the will has appeared to it in the world as representation. In this mirror the will knows itself in increasing degrees of distinctness and completeness, the highest of which is man."[3]

Humanness introduces personhood. At lower levels of life, up through nonhuman animal life, "individual character as a whole is lacking, since the species alone has a characteristic significance."[4] In nonhuman animal and plant life, the will to live exhibits and exerts itself at the species level. Survival of the species alone is meaningful. That is, perhaps, why the so-called "law of the jungle," as unpleasant as its manifestations may be, does not seem unjust to us when it operates at the nonhuman level. At the human level, however, with its highly developed capacity for individuated cognition and self-reflection, the will to live exhibits and exerts itself *not* at the species level, but at the level of the *individual:* "every person is to be

3. *WWR*-1, 274–75.
4. *WWR*-1, 132.

regarded as a specially determined and characterized phenomenon of the will."[5]

Schopenhauer referred to time and space as the *principium individuationis*.[6] The term easily transliterates itself into "principle of individuation." By "individuation," however, Schopenhauer really meant "plurality," in the sense of the one "individuated" into the many.[7] Individuation and plurality are synonymous in Schopenhauer's thought, and Schopenhauer's thought on individuality or plurality has a great deal to do with his understanding of the concept of justice. Justice, in Western legal systems, tends to be tinged with the individuated. It has a rights-and-entitlements focus.[8] In Eastern thought, however, justice tends to be identified with concepts like oneness, wholeness, and harmony.[9] Schopenhauer's understanding of justice is probably unique among Western philosophers. He identifies it, in Eastern fashion, with oneness and wholeness—a oneness and wholeness that he finds to be the true basis of reality itself. If Schopenhauer is correct, the Western focus on rights and entitlements as the basis of justice is not only erroneous, it is counterproductive and grossly misleading.

Our legal systems are so obviously built on the "rights-and-entitlements" sense of the concept of justice[10] that it would be difficult for us to grasp Schopenhauer's understanding of it, were he not so

---

5. *WWR*-1, 132.
6. *WWR*-1, 112.
7. *WWR*-2, 275. Psychologist Carl Jung, who was well read in Schopenhauer, used the term "individuation" in a different sense. Jung's "individuation" is a process of self-realization, and it more closely parallels Schopenhauer's doctrine of the denial of the will to live, discussed infra.
8. See, e.g., Raymond B. Marcin, "Justice and Love," *Catholic University Law Review* 33 (1984): 363.
9. One recalls Mohandas K. Gandhi's observation that "[t]hat action alone is just which does not harm either party to a dispute." Mohandas K. Gandhi, *The Collected Works of Mahatma Gandhi*, vol. 14 (New Delhi: Publications Division of the Government of India, 1958), 233 (hereinafter, Gandhi, *Collected Works*).
10. See chapter 16, "Modern Conceptions of Justice," infra.

blunt in expressing it. A rights-and-entitlements focus is premised on individuation and plurality—on the premise that each individual is an autonomous entity to which rights and entitlements can attach. Quite clearly, Schopenhauer consigns individuality and plurality to the world of phenomena. Individuality and plurality do not exist at the deep level of true reality. Remaining completely faithful to Kant's "Copernican Revolution," and thus regarding space and time as forms of our knowledge, that is, as impositions of the structures of our minds rather than as really existing objective entities, Schopenhauer went well beyond Kant and reasoned that the individuation (or plurality) that we see about us is possible only because of space and time. In reality, he reasoned, the "will" as the true thing-in-itself is *one*—not "one" in the sense of a single unit as opposed to a number of other units, but "one" in the sense that it lies outside space and time and therefore transcends the plurality that space and time alone make possible.

> [T]he will as thing-in-itself [wrote Schopenhauer] lies outside the principle of sufficient reason in all its forms, and is consequently completely groundless, although each of its phenomena is entirely subject to that principle. Further, it is free from all *plurality*, although its phenomena in time and space are innumerable. It is itself one, for the unity of an object is known in contrast to its possible plurality. Again, the will is one not as a concept is one, for a concept originates only through abstraction from plurality; but it is one as that which lies outside time and space, outside the *principium individuationis,* that is to say, outside the possibility of plurality. Only when all this has become quite clear to us . . . can we fully understand the meaning of the Kantian doctrine that time, space, and causality do not belong to the thing-in-itself, but are only forms of our knowing.[11]

11. *WWR*-1, 113 (emphasis in original).

Plurality (or individuation) according to Schopenhauer is just as subjective, just as "unreal," at the base level of reality, as space and time. It is at this point that Schopenhauer touches upon a metaphysics of justice. Traditional concepts of justice are based on the rights and entitlements of individuals or on how political systems can be organized in such a way that the rights and entitlements of individuals are secure. Schopenhauer's theory, at the deep level of true reality, prescinds from individuality itself. There are at that level no autonomous individualities to which rights and entitlements can attach. Consequently, justice as traditionally defined must be consigned and limited to the world of phenomena. There is no rights-and-entitlements justice at the deep level of true reality. There is only what Schopenhauer refers to as "eternal justice."

Chapter 9

The Inner Conflict

The world reflects the inner nature of the "will." In the human being, "will" comes to know its reflected nature. With this knowledge, "will" is, for the first time, called upon to do something—to react. In the human, "will" has to either affirm itself or deny itself. It of course affirms itself. But think—it affirms itself at the level of the individual human being. It is not affirming itself *in itself,* undifferentiated, unindividuated. At the level of the human being, the "will" or the will to live (Schopenhauer calls the "will to live" a mere "pleonasm," that is, a redundancy, of the "will")[1] comes into conflict with itself. Because every knowing individual is the *whole* will to live, every knowing individual, in a sense, makes himself the center of the world psychologically.[2] And this making of one's self the center of the world, this egoism, results in "the expression of the contradiction with which the will-to-live is affected in its inner self."[3] This inner conflict or contradiction of the will is a necessity.[4]

---

1. *WWR*-1, 275.   2. *WWR*-1, 332.
3. *WWR*-1, 333.
4. "[T]he will must live on itself, since nothing exists besides it, and it is a hun-

We see this pursuit—this striving, hunting, endless becoming—at the nonhuman level of living things, as the so-called "law of the jungle" or the "survival of the fittest." Animals and plants work to advance the will to live that is in them, and a destruction no less so than a survival comports with the will to live, because at the deep level of true reality, victim and predator are one. The one great will is feeding on itself, because there is nothing else to feed on; all *is* the will. When all this is transferred to the human level, Schopenhauer's theory of justice begins, and with it his understanding of the psychological and moral constitution of the human being, that is, his theory of right and wrong.

Right and Wrong

Schopenhauer's treatment of the moral concepts of right and wrong is essential to a correct understanding of his oft-misunderstood and therefore oft-ignored doctrine of the denial of the will to live. His theory of right and wrong is, moreover, important in its own context. It leads directly into his theories of property, of law, and of the state. Characteristically, Schopenhauer's theory of right and wrong is based squarely in his main metaphysical thesis that the world, that is, all of reality, is "will" and is also "representation." Recall his assertion that the noumenal underlying reality of the "will" is present whole and entire in each of its phenomena or manifestations, that is, in each individual:

> [T]he will will everywhere manifest itself in the plurality of individuals. This plurality, however, does not concern the will as thing-in-itself, but only its phenomena. The will is present, whole and undivided, in each of these, and perceives around it

---

gry will. Hence arise pursuit, hunting, anxiety, and suffering. . . . [T]he will in itself . . . is an endless striving. . . . Eternal becoming, endless flux, belong to the revelation of the essential nature of the will." *WWR*-1, 154, 164.

the innumerably repeated image of its own inner being; but this inner nature itself, and hence what is actually real, it finds immediately only in its inner self.[5]

In other words, the whole "will," the supremely inflated "will," is present in each of us, but not at the conscious level. This leads to the inflated egoism that we find rampant both in our selves (if we are honest enough to admit it) and in the world around us. Thomas Hobbes was correct: The world in which we find ourselves, stripped of civilizing law, is a *bellum omnium contra omnes*.[6]

All that being so, Schopenhauer reasons, it is easy for the will, individuated in a human being, affirming itself as it does in a given individual, to go beyond mere self-affirmation and into a *denial* of that very same will in others. Because of its inherent egoism and because of the fact that the individuated will is not immediately conscious of its own presence in other individuals, it is easy for the individuated will to assume an unwarranted attitude of centrality and self-importance, *all*-importance, and to engage in self-aggrandizing at the expense of another individual. The will in one individual *feeds on* the will (itself) in another. That, in Schopenhauer's understanding, is what is meant by a "wrong." "Wrong ... [Schopenhauer asserted] ... is most completely, peculiarly, and palpably expressed in cannibalism [i.e., the will feeding on itself in another form]."[7] A "wrong" exists whenever one human being extends his or her self-affirming will in such a way as to deny the self-affirming will in another human being. Schopenhauer himself explained it clearly: "[T]he content of the concept of *wrong* [is] that quality of an individual's conduct in which he extends the affirmation of the will that appears in

---

5. *WWR*-1, 331–32.
6. "War of all against all." Schopenhauer cited Hobbes approvingly at *WWR*-1, 331.
7. *WWR*-1, 335.

his own body so far that it becomes the denial of the will that appears in the bodies of others."[8]

Quite characteristically, in Schopenhauer's thought, *wrong* becomes the positive, and *right* the negative. A *right* is simply a moral claim not to have a *wrong* committed against one. As Schopenhauer put it, "there would be no talk of *right* if there were no wrong."[9] The "right of self-defense" would seem to be the original right out of which all contextual rights are derived. As Schopenhauer put it,

> [i]f an individual goes so far in the affirmation of his own will that he encroaches on the sphere of will-affirmation essential to my person as such, and denies this, then my warding off of that encroachment is only the denial of that denial, and to this extent is nothing more on my part than the affirmation of the will appearing essentially and originally in my body, and implicitly expressed by the mere phenomenon of this body; consequently it is not wrong and is therefore right.[10]

This theory of "right" leads to some interesting moral conclusions. If one is warding off an encroachment on the sphere of will-affirmation that is essential to his or her person as such, one has the "right" to do what might otherwise be considered morally wrong. That is, just as the person whose life or property is threatened with harm or injury has the right to use necessary force in defending them, so too would such a person have the right to *lie* to the wrongdoer.[11] Also, and at the other end of the moral spectrum, under Schopenhauer's quite libertarian concept of "wrong," it would not be "wrong" for a person to decline to assist another who is in dire need,

---

8. *WWR*-1, 339.   9. *WWR*-1, 339.
10. *WWR*-1, 339–40.
11. "I have an actual right to lie precisely to the extent that I have a right to compulsion." *WWR*-1, 340.

although Schopenhauer points out that such an uncharitable person would be quite likely in other contexts to commit genuine wrongs on others whenever such a person's desires demanded it.[12]

On the issue of property and property rights, Schopenhauer once again departed from his great mentor Kant. Kant, according to Schopenhauer, attempted to ground a right to property in "first occupation,"[13] which neatly supports a title and inheritance system. Schopenhauer, of course, had to fit the idea of property into his main thesis on the will and representation. To Schopenhauer, once property comes within the sphere of a person's affirmation of his or her individuated manifestation of the will, a moral right to property arises. How does an item of property achieve such a status, that is, how does it come within the sphere of a person's affirmation of his or her individuated manifestation of the will? By the productive expenditure of effort on the item of property. Schopenhauer quoted from the ancient Hindu *Laws of Manu* to make the point that "a cultivated field is the property of him who cut down the wood and cleared and plowed the land, just as an antelope belongs to the first hunter who mortally wounds it."[14]

Conscience

Notice that Schopenhauer's theory of "right" and "wrong" seems to operate only at the level of phenomena. Since the noumenal level of deep reality in which "will" itself holds sway is all but foreclosed to us, we have to operate at the level of phenomena, where the will to live (un*know*ingly) feeds on itself. That feeding could easily turn into a feeding *frenzy*; hence the need to recognize some moral principles that might control and discipline it. This observation could

---

12. *WWR*-1, 339.   13. *WWR*-1, 336.
14. *WWR*-1, 336, quoting from *Laws of Manu*, ix, 44. The *Laws of Manu* can be found on the Internet at "www.fordham.edu/halsall/india/manu-full.html."

lead the reader to conclude that Schopenhauer is about to discuss his doctrine of the state, but he is not yet ready for that. His stress at this point is on the adjective "moral": "[R]ight and wrong are merely *moral* determinations, i.e., such as have validity with regard to the consideration of human conduct as such, and in reference to the *inner significance of this conduct in itself.*"[15]

The control and discipline that are needed if the will's feeding on itself is not to become a cannibalistic, Hobbesian feeding frenzy come initially not from the state, but rather from *inside,* from a *consciousness* of "the inner significance of this conduct in itself [i.e., the fact that the will *is* feeding upon itself]." Here we are led to Schopenhauer's explanation of how it is that his main metaphysical thesis explains the occurrence of *conscience* in human beings:

> This [i.e., the "inner significance of this conduct in itself"] announces itself directly in consciousness by the fact that, on the one hand, the wrongdoing is accompanied by an inner pain, and this is the merely felt consciousness of the wrongdoer of the excessive strength of will-affirmation in himself which reaches the degree of denial of another's phenomenon of will, as also the fact that, as phenomenon, he is different from the sufferer of the wrong, but is yet in himself identical with him.[16]

The dual nature of all reality that defines Schopenhauer's main thesis is, according to Schopenhauer, what gives birth to *conscience* in the human being. Or, better stated, the human being's "*felt c*onsciousness" of the *excessiveness* of his or her will-affirmation activity is what "conscience" *is.* It is the *felt—not* really *known* in the certainty of the intellect—but merely *felt,* consciousness that the wrongdoer is "in himself identical with" his or her victim. It is that tiny bit of "felt consciousness" that we all have that at the level of deep reality all is one.

15. *WWR*-1, 341. 16. *WWR*-1, 341.

Chapter 10

A Brief Glimpse into Theistic Natural Law Theory

"Synderesis" in Aquinas and in Schopenhauer

Schopenhauer's very important doctrine of "conscience" contains elements that build upon the much older natural law tradition and even upon the biblical accounts on which that tradition is based.

The existence of conscience has always been difficult to explain in terms of philosophy. Saint Thomas Aquinas, the great natural law theorist and Doctor of the Church, located conscience in the human being's intellect. He also posited and identified a "habit" or inclination that activates and guides conscience, and he used an obscure philosophical term to express that habit or inclination. "Habit" *(habitus)* in Aquinas means something somewhat different from and much stronger than what it might mean in common parlance today. Aquinas used the word to signify a built-in inner inclination, not a course of action entrenched by repetition. He called this habit *"synderesis"* and regarded it as the "ignition spark" that activates *con-*

science and also as the direction finder that points conscience toward the "good." The habit or inclination of *synderesis*, according to Aquinas, exists in the intellect and always moves the intellect to direct the will[1] to choose *good* rather than evil. The word *"synderesis"* was apparently coined in Latin as *"synteresis"* by Saint Jerome, author of the Latin Vulgate edition of the Bible in the fourth century, A.D. Saint Jerome simply transliterated "synteresis" from a Greek word, συντερήσις, which in its verb form means to watch closely or to keep safe. In Greek συντερήσις is somewhat similar to the word meaning "conscience" itself, that is, συνειδήσις. Saint Jerome defined his usage of *synteresis* to mean the "spark of conscience" *(scintilla conscientiae)* that exists in all of us and that not even Cain's sin could eradicate from our nature.[2] In the sense in which Aquinas used the term, it becomes both the ignition spark that activates conscience and the direction-indicator that always points conscience toward the "good."

Aquinas, of course, had to deal with two obvious problems in connection with this idea of *synderesis*. One problem was that the notion *"good"* seems to beg the question. What is "good"? What is "evil"? That which may be good for one person in one circumstance is not necessarily good for another person or even for the same person in another circumstance. Moreover, ideological pluralism, even in Aquinas's day, and much more so in our own day, dictates that people can honestly disagree on what is "good" and what is not good. And that leads into the second obvious difficulty with Aquinas's concept of *synderesis*. People obviously do not always choose the "good";

---

1. Aquinas's "will," of course, is not the "will" of Schopenhauerian theory. Aquinas regarded the intellect, not the will, as the superior faculty in human beings. The will, for Aquinas, was simply the conventional idea of a choice-making faculty in the human being's make-up. For Schopenhauer, of course, the "will" is the ground of all being.

2. See Alan B. Wolter, *Duns Scotus on the Will and Morality* (Washington, D.C.: The Catholic University of America Press, 1986), 45.

people choose the "not-good" much of the time. Aquinas solved both problems, in his own mind at least, by differentiating between the *Good* and the *good*. Good with a capital "G," is God Himself, or God's will, that is, what God Himself would want us to choose. But Aquinas well knew that humanity was flawed due to the Fall of Adam, and its members did not invariably choose (or even know) what God would want them to choose. In other words, we often choose what pleases us rather than what pleases God. The Judeo-Christian concept of original sin, infecting all of us, is what makes us choose "good" with a small "g" much or most of the time. In Aquinas's words, we settle for the perishable good of this world instead of choosing the Imperishable Good that is God Himself.[3]

It is at this point that the nineteenth-century Schopenhauer touches the thirteenth-century Aquinas. Quite consistently with Aquinas, Schopenhauer accepted an understanding of original sin that involved a deep, ontological disorientation of human existence. One may perhaps view Schopenhauer's strong acceptance of the concept of original sin (albeit as an allegory, but as an allegory that explains a metaphysical reality in the human condition) as the formal source of his pessimism. Schopenhauer's words:

> The myth of the fall of man . . . is the only thing in the Old Testament to which I can concede a metaphysical, although only allegorical, truth; indeed, it is this alone that reconciles me to the Old Testament. Thus our existence resembles nothing but the consequence of a false step, and a guilty desire.[4]

If Aquinas's theory of conscience had a weakness, however, it was probably in the fact that he saw the need to posit such a thing as

---

3. Saint Thomas Aquinas, *Summa Theologiae*, Ia IIae q.82, a.3, trans. Fathers of the English Dominican Province under the title *Summa Theologica* (Allen, Tex.: Christian Classics, 1981), 2: 958 (hereinafter, Aquinas).

4. *WWR*-2, 580.

synderesis at all. He rightly saw the need for some igniting agent to activate conscience, but he failed to explain adequately why it is that conscience *pricks* us when we choose the perishable good instead of the Imperishable One. Perhaps implicit in Aquinas's thought is the fact that deep down in all of us is the knowledge of our own finiteness. We are not our own source. We are creatures, and we know that fact. And so, deep down, we know that there is a difference between our wants and our Creator's wants—but how is it, in Aquinas's thought, that we somehow know, despite original sin, what the Creator wants in a given situation?

Schopenhauer's *"Synderesis"*

It is at this point that Schopenhauer's theory of conscience may have an advantage. Despite the very relevant facts that Saint Thomas Aquinas was a bold and unapologetic theist and Arthur Schopenhauer was a bold and unapologetic atheist,[5] the analogies between Schopenhauer's theory and Aquinas's are there for the seeing. Original sin, in Schopenhauer's scheme, would be the world of phenomena itself, where the Schopenhauerian will is awkwardly individuated in each of us, and thus chooses, as it must, to feed on itself (in Aquinas's scheme, to choose the perishable good). When we go too far, however, and (in Schopenhauerian terms) in affirming our own will to live, deny another person's phenomenon of will to live, we have deep down a "felt consciousness" of the oneness—the identity—of ourselves and the victim of our wrongdoing, and that "felt consciousness" is what pricks us and makes us uncomfortable with our choice. This "felt consciousness" of the oneness and identity of ourselves and the victim of our wrongdoing may be thought of as the Schopenhauerian analogue to Aquinas's *synderesis*. This "felt consciousness"

5. See Magee, 53, 287.

(Schopenhauer, of course, nowhere uses the term *"synderesis"*) has no question-begging element in it and is quite focused; it is a felt consciousness of a simple fact, not a debatable notion of "good." It is the felt consciousness of the oneness and identity between ourselves and the victim of our wrongdoing. Aquinas, with his strong stress on the intellect as the controlling mechanism, and a less focused idea of *synderesis,* seems relegated to explaining the prick of conscience in terms of unexplained and ill-defined information provided by the intellect—Aquinas's notion of the "informed" conscience, giving substance to the notion of "good."

According to Aquinas, the proper end of the habit or inclination of *synderesis* is the *Summum Bonum,* the Highest Good, which he, of course, identified with God. Schopenhauer, interestingly, not only used the term *"summum bonum,"* he agreed with (while critiquing) the proposition that the s*ummum bonum* is the proper end toward which the will in a human being strives:

> [E]very good is essentially relative [wrote Schopenhauer]; for it has its essential nature only in its relation to a desiring will. Accordingly, *absolute good* is a contradiction; highest good, *summum bonum,* signifies the same thing, namely in reality a final satisfaction of the will, after which no fresh willing would occur; a last motive, the attainment of which would give the will an imperishable satisfaction. . . . [F]or the will there is no permanent fulfilment which completely and for ever satisfies its craving.[6]

This is, of course, a critique of the Thomistic position. For Aquinas, God is the *Summum Bonum* that satisfies the human will. For Schopenhauer, the will in the individual human being is insatiable. But there *is* a s*ummum bonum* in Schopenhauer's theory after all. The

6. *WWR*-1, 362.

will cannot ever be satisfied. Constant and continuous affirmation of the will is useless. What then? The *will* must *not* be *affirmed* at all; it must be *denied:*

> [I]f we wish to give an honorary, or so to speak an emeritus, position to an old expression that from custom we do not like entirely to discard [the "old expression" being the *"summum bonum"*], we may, metaphorically and figuratively, call the complete self-effacement and denial of the will, true will-lessness, which alone stills and silences forever the craving of the will; which alone gives that contentment which cannot again be disturbed; which alone is world-redeeming; and which we shall now consider at the conclusion of our whole discussion; the absolute good, the *summum bonum;* and we may regard it as the only radical cure for the disease against which all other good things, such as all fulfilled wishes and all attained happiness, are only palliatives, anodynes.[7]

The Thomistic Natural Law Tradition in General

We will see in a later chapter that Schopenhauer's main doctrine of the denial of the will to live also relies, to an appreciable extent, on some of the teachings of the great Christian mystics and mystical theologians. Those teachings themselves evolved out of the very strong theistic, specifically Christian natural law tradition exemplified in the writings of Saint Thomas Aquinas and his predecessors and successors.

Schopenhauer certainly was no theist. Neither was he a Christian. He was, in the popular sense of the term, an atheist.[8] One might

---

7. *WWR*-1, 341.
8. See Magee, 53, 287.

think that, being an atheist—and a misanthrope as well—Schopenhauer might have harbored an attitude of antipathy toward Christianity and religion in general. Like many other scholars and thinkers, however, including Tolstoy, his antipathy was only toward what might be called organized Christianity or organized religion, the religion of dogma. As we shall see, his own doctrine of the denial of the will to live exhibits anything but an antipathy toward religion writ broadly and even toward certain aspects of Christianity.

Moreover, although certainly not in the Christian tradition, Schopenhauer's theory of justice may be thought to share something with the Christian natural law tradition. His theory certainly has a "law of nature" focus, and it is difficult to think of any theory of justice outside either the Christian natural law tradition or outside of Schopenhauer's own theory that is an *ontology* of justice, that is, a study of justice as a facet of being and of reality itself, instead of a mere instrumentalism or epistemology of justice. In that context, it may be worthwhile to digress momentarily, and take a glance at the unapologetically *theistic* Christian natural law tradition as both a contrast to and a comparison with Schopenhauer's unapologetically *atheistic* thought. We have already seen one point of agreement between Aquinas and Schopenhauer, namely, an understanding of the concept of original sin that involves the recognition of a deep, ontological disorientation of human existence. This is an understanding that is, of course, not easily accepted in today's postmodern world. Indeed, a simple *theistic* approach to philosophy is not easily accepted in today's postmodern world. It might also be worthwhile to highlight some of the differences between today's postmodernism and the thinking of Aquinas.

Natural law theory is probably as old as human speculative and practical thinking. Even in its organized written form, it antedates the Christian natural law tradition, and indeed Christianity itself, by hundreds of years. It was the mainstay of Greek and Roman as well as Eastern political and legal thought.[9] Its Christianized form found expression in the philosophical writings of Saint Augustine and the early Christian scholastic philosophers.[10]

The great Christian natural law tradition, however, centers on the philosophy of Saint Thomas Aquinas. Aquinas's natural law theory, indeed his philosophical system in general, is openly, unashamedly, and unapologetically theistic, that is, centered on God (as is Augustine's).

An orientation centered on God is not, however, the starting point or even a focal point in today's postmodern political philosophy and jurisprudential thought. Quite the contrary. The starting premise and indeed the main focal point of the postmodern thinking that has come to dominate our society's public philosophy is, perhaps, best exemplified by Justice O'Connor's now well known description of the heart of constitutional *liberty:* "At the heart of liberty is the right to define *one's own* concept of existence, of meaning, of the universe, and of the mystery of human life."[11] The important thing in today's moral thinking, according to this postmodern view, is not reality *per se*, but rather "one's own" concept of reality. And, if we accept Justice O'Connor's very typical postmodern subjective humanism as valid, one has the constitutional right to *define* that reality for one's self.

There we have it—a public philosophy founded on a reality, or a

---

9. See, e.g., Anton-Hermann Chroust, "The Philosophy of Law of the Early Sophists," *American Journal of Jurisprudence* 20 (1975): 81; and "Natural Law and 'According to Nature' in Ancient Philosophy," *American Journal of Jurisprudence* 23 (1978): 73; and Joseph P. Maguire, "Plato's Theory of Natural Law," *Yale Classical Studies* 10 (1947): 151.

10. See, e.g., Anton-Hermann Chroust, "The Fundamental Ideas in Saint Augustine's Philosophy of Law," *American Journal of Jurisprudence* 18 (1973): 57.

11. Planned Parenthood of Southeastern Pennsylvania v. Casey, 505 U.S. 833, 851 (1992) (emphasis added).

more properly a set of individualized realities, divorced from objectivity itself and even from the *idea* of objective truth or objective reality. In a sense, taken to its logical conclusion, Justice O'Connor's dictum bespeaks a philosophical outlook either centering God in the human individual (or rather in each and every one of a chaotic gaggle of human individuals) or in recognizing the human individual as "god" (Who else has the right to define [His] own concept of existence, of meaning, of the universe, and of the mystery of human life?). This "god," however, must be a very uncomfortable "god," a "god" who is in potential conflict with innumerable other "gods" whose claims to rights to define existence, meaning, the universe—reality itself—are just as valid as one's own. In Schopenhauerian terms, Justice O'Connor's dictum—which is, of course, widely accepted in our postmodern society—well encapsulates the notion of the inflated egoism of the "will" individuated and centered in each of us, potentially and unknowingly feeding on itself in other individuals in a chaotic *bellum omnium contra omnes*.

Aquinas's philosophy recognizes and defends human *liberty*,[12] but, in contradistinction to both Justice O'Connor's postmodernism and Schopenhauer's atheism, it does not divorce that liberty from understandings of truth or reality or objectivity. Instead, Aquinas first grounds *reality* itself on logical proofs of the existence of the transcendent God,[13] and he then grounds *human liberty* in a system that accepts objective truth and reality. One should not be overly sanguine about the possibility of reconciling the two starting points—the postmodern, exemplified in Justice O'Connor's dictum and also exemplified in Schopenhauer's doctrine of the *affirmation* of the will to live on the one hand, and the Thomistic view on the other. They are fundamentally at odds, although as we shall see, the Thomistic view

12. See, Aquinas, Ia q.83, 1: 417–21.
13. See Aquinas, Ia q.2, a.3; 1:13–14.

coalesces to some extent (to the extent that theism *can* coalesce with atheism) with Schopenhauer's doctrine of the *denial* of the will to live.

So it is that Aquinas's philosophy and his theory of natural law is God centered. It is also rationalistic and realistic—based squarely on reason and intellect and on the conformity of intellectually perceived truth with objective reality. To put it simply, Aquinas believed that God is the transcendent Author of reality and that there are correct answers to moral problems, just as there are correct answers to speculative or mathematical problems. The answers, however, are not easy to come by. Aquinas recognized that the ultimate answers to all our problems—speculative as well as moral or practical—reside in the mind of God. Aquinas referred to these ultimate answers as the "eternal law" of God.[14] God exists in eternity. We exist in time. That is the nature of one of our dilemmas. God alone has the "Big Picture." Absent extraordinary divine revelation, we cannot possibly have a perfect understanding of the content of God's eternal law—the content of the mind of God. We can, however, have *an* understanding of God's eternal law—with our intellect and our reasoning capacity. Moreover, drawing both on divine revelation and on earlier Platonic philosophy, Aquinas recognized another aid. According to Aquinas, the moral requirements of God's eternal law are written on our hearts. Saint Paul put it this way:

> For when the Gentiles, who have not the law, do by nature those things that are of the law; these, having not the law, are a law to

---

14. Aquinas's "eternal law" is, in one sense, quite different from Schopenhauer's "eternal justice" (discussed infra; see chapter 11, "Eternal Justice"), i.e., in the sense that Aquinas locates his eternal law in the mind of God, and for Schopenhauer there is no God, but insofar as they both (Aquinas's "eternal law" and Schopenhauer's "eternal justice") present the "Ultima Thule" of all philosophy, the concepts are similar; for example, both posit an eternal law outside time and space.

themselves. Who shew [i.e., show] the work of the law *written in their hearts,* their conscience bearing witness to them; and their thoughts between themselves accusing or also defending one another.[15]

The suggestion that God's eternal law is somehow written on the human heart is not the exclusive province of Sacred Scripture. Aquinas and his predecessors in natural law theory recognized that sensibility in philosophy and they used that obscure philosophical term *synderesis*[16] to describe it. In Aquinas's natural law theory, *synderesis* formed a very important part of understandings of how we come to know the natural law. Just as the speculative intellect seems to have a natural built-in bent toward the *truth,* the practical intellect seems to have a natural built-in bent toward the *good,* and that natural built-in bent toward the good is what Aquinas meant by *"synderesis."*

This *"synderesis"* is *not* a synonym for "conscience" in Thomistic natural law theory. Conscience, in Thomistic theory, is a moral judging function; *synderesis* is a natural in-born inclination that is prior to the workings of conscience. In Thomistic natural law theory, *synderesis* is both the ignition spark that activates the moral conscience and its guide. How *synderesis* works in the area of moral decision-making is perhaps best exemplified by drawing an analogy to the way in which the speculative or mathematical intellect works. Recall your high school algebra and consider this step-by-step math problem:

1. Equation $\quad\quad\quad\quad\quad\quad\quad\quad\quad\quad a = b$
2. Multiply both sides by a $\quad\quad\quad\quad a^2 = ab$
3. Subtract b^2 from both sides $\quad\quad a^2 - b^2 = ab - b^2$

---

15. Romans 2:14–15 (Douay-Rheims) (emphasis added).
16. See Aquinas, Ia q.79, a.12; 1: 407.

4. Factor down	$(a+b)(a-b) = b(a-b)$
5. Divide both sides by (a–b)	$a+b = b$
6. Recall that a=b; substitute b for a	$b+b = b$
7. Add b+b	$2b = b$
8. Divide both sides by b	$2 = 1$

The result of this problem leaves our intellect in a state of speculative discomfort. Two cannot equal one, and yet the problem seems to have yielded that result.

It is the same, Aquinas said, with the practical intellect. We sometimes work out *moral* problems in such a way that our moral or practical intellect is left in a state of discomfort. Schopenhauer, too, recognized a state of discomfort in his doctrine of conscience—the discomfort that pricks us with the deep down, subconscious knowledge that the "will" that we are affirming in our moral decision making is the same "will" that inhabits the person who is affected by our decision. Returning to the thought of Aquinas, just as the built-in *principle of contradiction* tells us that something has gone wrong with our speculative or mathematical thinking, so too the built-in principle of *synderesis* tells us that something has gone wrong with our practical or moral thinking and thereby activates our "conscience" function.[17]

In the history of ideas, the philosophical concept of *synderesis* antedates Aquinas and is indeed older than Christian philosophy. Plato used it under a different name; he called it *anamnesis*. Platonic *anamnesis* connoted a built-in "remembrance" of the perfect Platonic Forms or Archetypes, including the Form or Idea or Archetype of

---

17. For the purpose of analysis and examples, Aquinas often separated the intellect into the speculative (dealing with mathematical and scientific reasoning) and the practical (dealing with moral reasoning), but he was very clear in declaring that the speculative intellect and the practical intellect are one and the same intellect. Only their ends distinguish the speculative and the practical. Aquinas, Ia q.79, a.11; 1: 406.

the Good. Although Schopenhauer never used the term *synderesis* or for that matter *anamnesis,* the concept of a built-in "remembrance" of the Platonic Idea well comports with Schopenhauer's "felt consciousness" of the oneness of the will. Pope Benedict XVI, when he was Prefect for the Congregation for the Doctrine of the Faith, said that he found the term *anamnesis* more useful in Catholic natural law thinking than the term *synderesis*.[18] By whatever term it is known, *synderesis* is, according to Aquinas, our practical intellect's "principle of contradiction," the built-in tendency that keeps us oriented toward the good in our quest for correct moral answers and that pricks us with discomfort when we depart from that orientation by doing something like the moral equivalent of dividing by zero (the defect in our mathematical example, committed in reaching step 5).

That *synderesis* really exists can be observed in how our culture handles controversial moral issues. One good example involves what Pope John Paul II called our present-day "culture of death," a remark that implicates (and indicts) the view represented by Justice O'Connor's postmodern subjective humanism, and does so in the context of the very moral and legal problem that Justice O'Connor was addressing when she wrote her dictum. Few will doubt that we sometimes do *evil* in the name of good. It is not difficult to concede, in charity, that Justice O'Connor, in pronouncing our society's allegiance to moral relativism, and the other justices, in continuing to uphold the "right" to kill those whom the Pope would regard as preborn babies, are sincere in their belief that they are accomplishing a social "good," that is, the upholding of the concept of liberty and personal autonomy in the context of the rights of the pregnant woman. It is not difficult to concede in charity that Pope John Paul II and all who follow his pro-life teachings are sincere in their belief that they

---

18. Joseph Cardinal Ratzinger (Pope Benedict XVI), "Conscience and Truth" 6 (paper presented at the 10th workshop for bishops, Dallas, Tex., February 1991).

too are accomplishing a social "good," namely, the upholding of the right to life of the most vulnerable and the most defenseless members of the human community.

Those two contrasting views suggest a problem for natural law theory. Natural law theory in general and *synderesis* in particular must, according to Aquinas, never be studied apart from a complete acceptance of the doctrine of original sin.[19] In human terms, the problem is that understandings of the "good" differ among human beings. In theological and straightforwardly biblical terms, before Adam's Fall, the *synderesis* in us was oriented toward "the Good" with a capital "G," that is, God Himself and God's own good for us. After the Fall, the *synderesis* within us is oriented toward "the good," that is, our own often flawed but seldom tentative understandings of "good." According to Thomistic doctrine, our wills are weakened and our intellects are darkened, such that we cannot no longer agree among ourselves on the true or the good. Ideological pluralism dooms any approach to the natural law that is not centered on God but instead is centered on humankind's own weak and flawed understanding of humankind's own nature.

Letting God, the Author of nature, into the moral equation (as Aquinas would surely do) enables the human mind to reach a deeper level of understanding—the understanding (to stay with the context in which Justice O'Connor formulated her definition of "liberty," but to reach a different result) that fetuses are *God's* children, indeed God's *littlest* children, with *their own* God-given rights to privacy, personal autonomy, and life itself.

Although *synderesis* and conscience are not identical in Thomistic thought, the connection between *synderesis* and conscience is obvious. Thomist theologian William E. May has referred to *synderesis*

---

19. Aquinas, Ia IIae q. 91, a.6; 2: 1000.

as the general as opposed to the particularized moral conscience, "our habitual awareness of the first principles of practical reasoning and of morality."[20] If *synderesis* is a built-in awareness of the first principles of moral reasoning, what, indeed, *are* those "first principles of moral reasoning" of which we are habitually aware and toward which we are inclined? What is the equivalent of the principle of contradiction for the the practical or moral intellect? Those questions lead us directly to the *content* of the natural law, the version of God's eternal law that is, in Saint Paul's words, "written on our hearts."

Aquinas, in assessing the general content of the natural law, began with a self-evident first principle. Just as "truth" is the first principle in the speculative intellect, so too "good" is the first principle of the practical or moral intellect. Aquinas put it this way: "[T]he first principle in the practical reason is one founded on the notion of good, viz., that *good is that which all things seek after.* Hence this is the first precept of law, that *good is to be done and pursued, and evil is to be avoided.*"[21] That first principle, it must be admitted, is question begging in the extreme, especially in the context of today's moral relativism. What *is* "good"? What *is* "evil"?[22]

Aquinas proceeded to take some of the question begging out of the first principle of natural law. He began to answer our questions by putting some content into the notion of "good." Aquinas listed three sets of "precepts" of the law of nature, dividing them into the

20. William E. May, *An Introduction to Moral Theology*, rev. ed. (Huntington, Ind.: Our Sunday Visitor Publishing Division, 1994), 33 (hereinafter, May).
21. Aquinas, Ia IIae q.94, a.2; 2:1009 (emphasis in original).
22. The difficulty today is the prevalence of the view that anyone's concept of what is good is as morally worthy as anyone else's. Such a proposition almost seems to be accepted as a given in today's moral discourse. Since one of the basic premises of Aquinas's rationalism and realism is that there is an objectively correct answer to each moral dilemma, that postmodern view is definitely not a given in Aquinas's natural law theory.

precepts that human beings have in common with all existing substances, those they have in common with nonrational animals, and those they share in common *because* they are rational beings.

(1) All existing substances hold onto existence; so too do human beings. Schopenhauer also used this starting point in one of his explanations of "will," characteristically starting not with the lowest of existing substances but rather with the highest: "If we consider the will where no one denies it, namely in knowing beings, we find everywhere, as its fundamental effort, the *self-preservation* of every being: *Omnis natura vult esse conservatrix sui* [translated in a footnote as "every being in nature endeavors to preserve itself"].[23] Schopenhauer then reasoned down from knowing beings to inanimate things held together by "gravitation," concluding that even inanimate objects were "a manifestation of the will's fundamental effort in all its phenomena, the impulse to self-preservation, which shows itself as the essential element even at the lowest stage."[24]

(2) All animals, by nature, do certain things. Aquinas listed two specifically: sexual intercourse and education of offspring.

(3) The complexity of reason has its input into the precepts of the natural law, in the form of a natural inclination to know the truth about God and to live amicably in society.

These are Aquinas's words:

> [A]ccording to the order of natural inclinations, is the order of the precepts of the natural law. Because in man there is first of all an inclination to good in accordance with the nature which he has in common with all substances: inasmuch as every substance seeks the preservation of its own being, according to its

---

23. *WWR*-2, 298. Aquinas worded the principle quite similarly: "[E]very substance seeks the preservation of its own being, according to its nature." Aquinas, Ia IIae q.94, a. 2; 2: 1009.

24. *WWR*-2, 298–99.

nature: and by reason of this inclination, whatever is a means of preserving human life, and of warding off its obstacles, belongs to the natural law. Secondly there is in man an inclination to things that pertain to him more specially, according to that nature which he has in common with other animals: and in virtue of this inclination, those things are said to belong to the natural law, *which nature has taught to all animals,* such as sexual intercourse, education of offspring and so forth. Thirdly, there is in man an inclination to good, according to the nature of his reason, which nature is proper to him: thus man has a natural inclination to know the truth about God, and to live in society: and in this respect, whatever pertains to this inclination belongs to the natural law; for instance, to shun ignorance, to avoid offending those among whom one has to live, and other such things regarding the above inclination.[25]

Thomist theologian William E. May has nicely summarized Aquinas's precepts of the law of nature as follows: "life itself, the handing on and education of life, true knowledge about God, [and] life in fellowship and amity with others."[26]

With those precepts as starting points, Aquinas called upon the poser of a moral dilemma to reason his or her way to the correct moral answer. In Aquinas's natural law theory, however, the task of the poser of the moral dilemma is nothing less than a quest to touch the mind of God. Recall the role of *"synderesis"* in Aquinas's natural law theory, discussed earlier. Professor May put it this way: "[N]atural law . . . is the way human beings *actively* participate in the divine law, ordering their own actions in accordance with this law insofar as this law is inwardly known by them."[27] The quest for the correct

25. Aquinas, Ia IIae q.94, a.2; 2:1009.
26. May, 49.
27. May, 60 (emphasis in original).

moral answer, in other words, *has* something "inner" about it, but it is *not* an inner quest for one's *own* deepest feelings or one's *own* deeply felt values.[28] It is instead a quest to discover, with the intellect and reason given us by our Creator and with the aid of synderesis, that spark of God's eternal law that exists in each of His rational creatures, the true, objective moral reality. That point is very important. It is the point at which classic natural law theory departs from today's postmodern subjectivism. In Aquinas's system personal *sin* may have a *sub*jective element to it, but *moral principles* have true *ob*jective reality. Aquinas is no moral relativist or moral subjectivist.

It must be acknowledged that natural law theory is much older than Aquinas; it is even much older than Christianity. It was *the* foundational jurisprudence of the Western mindset. From one vantage point, it may be said that what Aquinas and his Catholic predecessors did was to "baptize" natural law jurisprudence into theism in general and Christianity in particular, but perhaps the better way of looking at it is to observe that Aquinas (and Augustine and all the other Christian predecessors of Aquinas) completed the very much incomplete natural law theory of the ancient Greek philosophers by recognizing the role of the Author of nature in the formation and formulation of its principles. Professor Anton-Hermann Chroust of Notre Dame once wrote:

> The philosophy of law of St. Thomas is without doubt the embodiment of a great tradition—a tradition which proceeded from Greek and Roman thought and subsequently was welded to Christianity. The merits inherent in this jurisprudence are beyond question. The views of St. Thomas about law and justice,

---

28. Aquinas's treatment of original sin and its aftermath gives an indication why such a quest for one's *own* inner moral sensibilities is not likely to succeed. See Aquinas, Ia IIae qq.82, 83, and 85; 2: 956–62 and 966–71.

especially in matters concerning the relationship of law and morals and the necessity of referring the law to some ultimate objective standard beyond the law, have become a deathless legacy for all meaningful jurisprudential theories.[29]

29. Anton-Hermann Chroust, "The Philosophy of St. Thomas Aquinas: His Fundamental Ideas and Some of His Historical Precursors," *American Journal of Jurisprudence* 19 (1974): 1, 37–38.

Chapter 11

Eternal Justice

[I]n all that happens or indeed can happen to the individual, justice is always done to it.[1]

We return now to Schopenhauer's decidedly nontheistic philosophy, and to his doctrine of the affirmation of the will-to-live. Transferred to the human level, the affirmation of the will to live, the so-called "law of the jungle," is usually regarded as socially inappropriate, even morally wrong. In that context, then, Schopenhauer's theory of justice deals directly and intensely with what philosophy and theology refer to as the problem of evil. In most systems of ethics and in most systems of moral theology, the problem of evil is a stumbling block, or even an embarrassment, but not in Schopenhauer's, and its solution lies at the very heart of his metaphysics.[2] Most systems either founder or else wallow in circumlocutions when they

1. *WWR*-1, 351.
2. See *WWR*-2, 643.

confront the fact of the existence of evil in the world and try to reconcile it with either an all-good God or with the supposed essential goodness of human nature. The problem is impossible to avoid and must be confronted in any system of ethics. Schopenhauer recognizes it in our common, everyday experience that "sees the wicked man, after misdeeds and cruelties of every kind, live a life of pleasure, and quit the world undisturbed. It sees the oppressed person drag out to the end a life full of suffering without the appearance of an avenger or vindicator."[3]

The conventional explanation, remarkably consistent over the centuries and across many cultures, posits a judgment after death in which the oppressor receives his or her "comeuppance" and the oppressed his or her reward. In contemporary times, that explanation seems not to be wearing well, and a century and a half ago it ill suited Schopenhauer, who quoted Euripides to impugn it:

> Do you think that crimes ascend to the gods on wings, and then someone has to record them there on the tablet of Jove, and that Jove looks at them and pronounces judgement on men? The whole of heaven would not be great enough to contain the sins of men, were Jove to record them all, nor would he to review them and assign to each his punishment. No! the punishment is already there, if only you will see it.[4]

Schopenhauer's explanation is intriguing: "[T]he punishment is already there, if only you will see it." What Schopenhauer means may become clearer if we take a slight and brief digression.

---

3. *WWR*-1, 353–354.
4. *WWR*-1, 351, n. 45. The quoted language is from Euripides, Stobaeus, *Eclog.*, I, c.4.

Schopenhauer and Gandhi

Earlier in this study, it was mentioned that Schopenhauer was Adolf Hitler's favorite philosopher.[5] It is a strange irony that Schopenhauer may have had a limited and indirect influence on the thought of Hitler's contemporary and his moral antithesis, Mohandas K. Gandhi, the sainted Mahatma of India. It is no secret that Gandhi was greatly influenced by the religious and moral writings of the writer Leo Tolstoy.[6] It is perhaps less well known that Tolstoy was quite familiar with the philosophy of Schopenhauer.[7] That is not to say that Gandhi necessarily took some philosophical principles from Schopenhauer, even indirectly. Whatever principles Gandhi could have taken indirectly from Schopenhauer were more directly and more readily available in Gandhi's own native Hinduism and in his understandings of the essence of the Christianity to which he had been exposed. It is merely to suggest that there may be a consonance between the thoughts of the man who did not practice what he preached and the man who did, with Tolstoy's thought providing the resonance. The sympathetic vibrations are nowhere clearer than in the solutions each propounded to the problem of evil.

Schopenhauer's solution to the problem of evil is presaged quite

---

5. See, e.g., Payne, 115; Toland, 85; and Fest, 69, 200. Very likely the attractiveness of Schopenhauer's thought to Adolf Hitler lay in the reasons it was attractive to Richard Wagner. Schopenhauer's understanding of the Platonic Ideas led to a very strong and liberating theory of aesthetics which Wagner, his contemporary, heartily embraced, and which, a century later, gave a feeling of vindication to Hitler who never accepted his failures as an artist and architect. It is a grievously lamentable tragedy of history that Hitler did not find a similar attractiveness in Schopenhauer's theory of justice with its stress on the value of compassion. See Magee, 350–69, for an account of Schopenhauer's influence on Wagner.

6. See, e.g., Gandhi, Mohandas K., *An Autobiography: The Story of My Experiments With Truth*, trans. Mahadev Desai (first published in two volumes in 1927 and 1929 in the Gujarati language) (Boston: Beacon Press, 1957), 137–38 (hereinafter, Gandhi, *Autobiography*).

7. See Magee, 403–4.

clearly in his metaphysics. Recall that for Schopenhauer the true reality, that is, the thing-in-itself of everything, is "will." And human knowledge of the "outside world" is conditioned by the structure of the human mind, which imposes time, space, and the principle of causality on all its perceptions of the outside world. Time, space, and causality do not exist in the thing-in-itself. Only timeless, spaceless, and causeless "will" exists. Consequently the "will" is undivided, that is, there is a basic, very real unity among all existence, a wholeness to all that exists. We are more than our brother's keeper. In the most basic ontological sense, we *are* our brother. Schopenhauer applies all this to the problem of evil:

> [T]he difference between the inflicter of suffering and he who must endure it is only phenomenon, and does not concern the thing-in-itself which is the will that lives in both. Deceived by the knowledge bound to its service, the will here fails to recognize itself; seeking enhanced well-being in *one* of its phenomena, it produces great suffering in *another*. Thus in the fierceness and intensity of its desire it buries its teeth in its own flesh, not knowing that it always injures only itself, revealing in this form through the medium of individuation the conflict with itself which it bears in its inner nature. Tormentor and tormented are one. The former is mistaken in thinking that he does not share the torment, the latter in thinking he does not share the guilt.[8]

Gandhi too wrote about the problem of evil, which he discussed in terms of *"himsa,"* a Hindi word carrying the connotation of violent harm or killing.

---

8. *WWR*-1, 354.

We are helpless mortals caught in the conflagration of *himsa*.
The saying that life lives on life has a deep meaning. . . . Man
cannot for a moment live without consciously or unconsciously
committing outward *himsa*. . . . [B]ecause underlying *ahimsa*
(i.e., nonviolence) is the unity of all life, the error of one cannot
but affect all, and hence man cannot be wholly free from
himsa.[9]

Life lives on life and yet all life is one. Gandhi and Schopenhauer both held to that proposition. And the lesson that Schopenhauer drew (that "tormentor and tormented are one") but did not put into practice is the lesson that Gandhi also drew, and did indeed put into practice, with society-altering results. For the success of his technique of nonviolent resistance Gandhi banked on that very principle, namely, that deep down, at some unfathomable level, tormentor and tormented are one and that by accepting the torment (more than that — by willingly seeking it out), the tormented can somehow bring the tormentor to that realization.[10]

Schopenhauer, perhaps because he had the luxury of not having to put his theory of justice into practice, drew a conclusion that Gandhi never seemed able to communicate to his followers and which, perhaps, prevented Gandhi's theories from stemming the violence that accompanied the partition of India and Pakistan, a partition in which both Hindus and Muslims were able to view themselves with equal justification as oppressed victims.[11] The conclusion that Schopenhauer drew (and that Gandhi had difficulty communicating) was this: Not only does the tormentor, at that deep ontological level, share the *torment*, but the tormented, at that same level,

9. Gandhi, *Autobiography*, 349.
10. *WWR*-1, 365.
11. See, e.g., Larry Collins and Dominique LaPierre, *Freedom at Midnight* (New York: Avon, 1975).

shares the *guilt.* At the level of true reality, tormentor and tormented *are one and the same.* If the tormented shares the guilt, Schopenhauer is quite correct in reaching the otherwise cryptic conclusion that "in all that happens or indeed can happen to the individual, justice is always done to it."[12] This is Schopenhauer's doctrine of eternal justice. It is the "will" feeding on itself. In Gandhi's thought it is the violent "conflagration of *himsa,*" in which "life lives on life."

It is well known, however, that Gandhi's understanding of the Hindu concept of *himsa* (i.e., violence) led him to a doctrine of *"a-himsa"* (i.e., *non*violence) and through that to a positive and remarkable state of holiness and wholeness. Gandhi clearly viewed the "conflagration of *himsa*" (Schopenhauer's unchecked affirmation of the will to live) as something to be striven against. One cannot envision Gandhi choosing the term "eternal justice" to express the "conflagration of *himsa,*" but Schopenhauer did use the term "eternal justice," and in doing so was suggesting that it, or an understanding of it, was something to be sought and even embraced as something that can lead to "virtue":

> [E]ternal justice will be grasped and comprehended only by the man who rises above that knowledge which proceeds on the guiding line of the principle of sufficient reason and is bound to individual things, who recognizes the Ideas, who sees through the *principium individuationis,* and who is aware that the forms of the phenomenon do not apply to the thing-in-itself. Moreover, it is this man alone who, by dint of the same knowledge, can understand the true nature of virtue, . . . although for the practice of virtue this knowledge in the abstract is by no means required.[13]

12. *WWR*-1, 351.
13. *WWR*-1, 354.

Seeing, grasping, and accepting "eternal justice" leads to an understanding of the true nature of virtue. Schopenhauer explained how this understanding comes about:

> [T]he most fundamental of all our errors is that, with reference to one another, we are not-I. On the other hand, to be just, noble, and benevolent is nothing but to translate my metaphysics into actions. To say that time and space are mere forms of our knowledge, not determinations of things-in-themselves, is the same as saying that the teaching of metempsychosis, namely that "one day you will be born again as the man whom you now injure, and will suffer the same injury," is identical with the frequently mentioned formula of the Brahmans, *Tat tvam asi*, "This thou art." All genuine virtue proceeds from the immediate and *intuitive* knowledge of the metaphysical identity of all being.[14]

This very same passage deeply impressed famed quantum physicist Erwin Schrödinger:

> [I]nconceivable as it seems to ordinary reason [wrote Schrödinger], you—and all other conscious beings as such—are all in all. Hence this life of yours which you are living is not merely a piece of the entire existence, but is in a certain sense the *whole;* only this whole is not so constituted that it can be surveyed in one single glance. This, as we know, is what the Brahmins express in that sacred, mystic formula which is yet really so simple and so clear: *Tat tvam asi*, this is you.[15]

---

14. *WWR*-2, 600–1.
15. See Schrödinger, 21–22 (emphasis in original).

Brahman spirituality developed, of course, within the Hindu tradition, but this "Brahman" understanding of "eternal justice," seemingly shared by Schopenhauer, Gandhi, and Schrödinger, is really a staple of Eastern religious thought in general and Buddhist and Taoist thought in particular. According to the historian of religion Anesaki,

> [t]he central idea in Buddhist teaching is the gospel of universal salvation based on the idea of the fundamental oneness of all beings. There are in the world, Buddhism teaches, manifold existences and innumerable beings, and each of these individuals deems himself to be a separate being and behaves accordingly. But in reality they make up one family, there is one continuity throughout, and this oneness is to be realized in the attainment of Buddhahood on the part of each and all, in the full realization of the universal communion. Individuals may purify themselves and thereby escape the miseries of sinful existence, yet the salvation of anyone is imperfect so long as and so far as there remain any who have not realized the universal spiritual communion, i.e., who are not saved. To save oneself by saving others is the gospel of universal salvation taught by Buddhism.[16]

The Taoist tradition is in accord. Max Kaltenmark explained the thought of the Taoist philosopher Chuang Tsu, and in doing so echoed Schopenhauer's doctrine of "eternal justice":

> If we start from the principle that all things and creatures (men included) are fundamentally identical, i.e., are one, then we

---

16. Quoted in E. A. Burtt, *The Teachings of the Compassionate Buddha* (New York: Mentor Books, 1955), 124. Anesaki was writing about the particularly activist and well-developed form of Buddhism known as the Mahayana tradition, in which those who achieve enlightenment do not withdraw into themselves, but rather act on their newly discovered "oneness" by proselytizing others.

cannot legitimately pass judgment on them; we cannot approve of some and condemn others. Confrontations of opposed sets of opinions take place when people have lost their sense of universality: each side is blind to all but its own small parcel of self-interested truths, which it takes for the absolute.... However, as Lao Tzu demonstrates, affirmations and negations never fail to give rise to one another: if I am right, my neighbor must be wrong, and since my neighbor is equally convinced that he is right and I am wrong, the evil is without a cure; for we each cling to our own set of prejudices.... This means that we each have a particular self that we oppose to the selves of others. Yet within each of us there is a "Supreme Master" superior to all these distinctive particularisms, which arise from our viscera.... The Supreme Master is, of course, the Tao, the principle of life and unity....[17]

The "Tao" to Schopenhauer, would, of course, be the "will" at the deep level of reality-in-itself.

The Affirmation of the Will to Live

The fact that there is such a vast difference between the world as it appears phenomenally and the world as it really is—between the world as appearance and the world as thing-in-itself—between the world as representation and the world as will—creates a strange and difficult situation. The world as thing-in-itself affirms itself; it goes about its existential task, and this activity, as it were, goes on behind the scenes of the world of appearances. Viewed from the world of appearances, this activity is subject to time, space, causality, plurality,

17. Max Kaltenmark, *Lao Tzu and Taoism*, trans. Roger Greaves (Stanford, Calif.: Stanford University Press, 1965), 75.

all the limitations and conditions imposed by the structure of the perceiving mind. In this context the will manifests itself as self-affirmation. But recall, plurality applies only to the world of appearance. The entire "will" exists in each apparently individual entity. Schopenhauer expressed it thusly:

> [T]he will will everywhere manifest itself in the plurality of individuals. This plurality, however, does not concern the will as thing-in-itself, but only its phenomena. The will is present, whole and undivided, in each of these, and perceives around it the innumerably repeated image of its own inner being; but this inner nature itself, and hence what is actually real, it finds immediately only in its inner self.[18]

This situation naturally leads to the egoism that we saw earlier— the egoism that Schopenhauer posits as the all-pervasive original motivation in human beings. This self-affirmation in the plant and animal world appears in the all too familiar "law of the jungle," with predator affirming itself at the expense of prey. At the human level, it assumes moral proportions in Hobbes's *bellum omnium contra omnes*.[19] As we have seen, Schopenhauer finds in this individuated self-affirmation not only the source of egoism, but also the source of "wrong."

> [S]ince the will manifests that *self-affirmation* of one's own body in innumerable individuals beside one another, in one individual, by virtue of the egoism peculiar to all, it very easily goes beyond this affirmation to the *denial* of the same will appearing in another individual.... This breaking through the boundary of another's affirmation of will has at all times been distinctly rec-

---

18. *WWR*-1, 331–32.
19. Schopenhauer heartily endorsed Hobbes's thesis. *WWR*-1, 333.

ognized, and its concept has been denoted by the word *wrong* (*Unrecht*).[20]

"Wrong" is, thus, in Schopenhauer's thought, the norm and "right" the exception, or as he puts it "the concept of *wrong* is the original and positive; the opposite concept of *right* is the derivative and negative.... The concept of *right* contains merely the negation of wrong."[21]

20. *WWR*-1, 334.
21. *WWR*-1, 339.

Chapter 12

The Denial of the Will to Live

Because of the way in which it manifests itself in the world of appearances, that is, the world as represented to us through the structures of our perceiving mind (time, space, causality, plurality, etc.) the "will," which at the human level Schopenhauer refers to as the "will to live," is involved in a delusion. The "will" as thing-in-itself, is (as has been indicated) something like tendency or probability. There is no clear word for it because it is a transcendent concept. Schopenhauer calls it endless, aimless, limitless striving. In that sense, it is a tendency without an aim, other than that of eternal becoming or flux. The "will" as represented to the perceiving mind, however, is seen as a will to live. The perceiving mind cannot understand an aimless tendency, and so it separates will into two thoughts. In reality, the tendency *is* the existence. The perceiving mind, however, records it as a tendency *to* exist, hence, as a will-to-*live*.[1] Despite the countless individuals who inhabit the world, the will to live

---

1. See *WWR*-1, 162–165, 275; and *WWR*-2, 349–60.

is unindividuated and is present, whole and entire, in each individual. Moreover, it seeks to affirm itself in this delusional milieu, often at the expense of itself.

The delusional milieu in which the will finds itself is not unknown in the cultural traditions that have developed over the years. Schopenhauer sees it in both Christianity and Hinduism. In Christianity, this delusion takes the form of the doctrine of original sin. Quoting the poet Calderon who wrote ". . . man's greatest offence is that he has been born," Schopenhauer concludes "[i]n that verse Calderon has merely expressed the Christian dogma of original sin."[2] In Hinduism, Schopenhauer found this delusional milieu in the doctrine of the veil of *Maya:*

> [T]he ancient wisdom of the Indians declares that "it is Mâyâ, the veil of deception, which covers the eyes of mortals, and causes them to see a world of which one cannot say either that it is or that it is not. . . ."
>
> . . .
>
> [I]t is . . . individuation that keeps the will-to-live in error as to its own true nature; it is the *Maya* of Brahmanism.[3]

Both religious traditions, of course, provide a solution for the human being's predicament, and both employ the same word when they discuss their solutions: salvation. But the word "salvation" on the lips of the average Christian means something quite different from what it means on the lips of a Brahman. Christian salvation traditionally accommodates and preserves the individuality of the saved person. Hindu salvation does not; in fact in Hindu philosophy (carried over into and developed more fully in Buddhism), existence itself is transcended in the state known as Nirvana (a word which is

---

2. See *WWR*-1, 355.
3. *WWR*-1, 8; and *WWR*-2, 601.

somewhat paradoxically but correctly translated both as "enlightenment" and as "extinction").[4]

In the final analysis, Schopenhauer's "salvation" is much closer to the Hindu/Buddhist than to the traditional Christian understanding, although he couches it more often than not in Christian terminology. For example: "The doctrine of original sin (*affirmation* of the will) and of salvation (*denial* of the will) is really the great truth which constitutes the kernel of Christianity.... Accordingly, we should interpret Jesus Christ always in the universal, as the symbol of personification of the denial of the will-to-live...."[5]

Salvation, for Schopenhauer, lies in the *denial* of the will to live, but this should not be understood superficially. Thinking simplistically, it would seem that the clearest and most direct route to salvation, in Schopenhauer's mind, would be suicide. Suicide seems at first glance to involve a denial of the will to live. But Schopenhauer very clearly held to the contrary. Suicide, according to Schopenhauer, involves an affirmation and not a denial of the will-to-live:

> The suicide wills life, and is dissatisfied merely with the conditions on which it has come to him. Therefore, he gives up by no means the will-to-live, but merely life, since he destroys the individual phenomenon.... [S]uicide ... is a quite futile and foolish act, for the thing-in-itself remains unaffected by it.... [I]t is also the masterpiece of Maya as the most blatant expression of the contradiction of the will-to-live with itself.[6]

True salvation, that is, true denial of the will to live, involves the "will" itself doing something about the "veil of *Maya*." It is not simply a matter of the "saved" individual choosing to ignore the delusion in-

---

4. See Heinrich Zimmer, *Philosophies of India*, ed. J. Campbell (Princeton, N.J.: Princeton University Press, 1951), 183, 448, 478–80, 666.
5. *WWR*-1, 405.
6. *WWR*-1, 398–99.

volved in the apparent plurality of things in the world. As we shall see below, in Schopenhauer's thought the individual human being has no free will and therefore cannot make such a choice. The only thing that has "free will" in Schopenhauer's scheme of things is the "will" itself, *as* thing-in-itself. Since, in the usual course of the world, the will is constantly involved in affirming itself in individual phenomena, most often at the expense of itself in other individual phenomena, the will is constantly "sinking its teeth into its own flesh." The alternative to this unpleasant state of affairs is for the will to deny itself—note: not for the individual human being to deny the will, but for the *will* itself to deny *itself,* to become quiescent, to cease its aimless striving. This event—the will denying itself—can occur in the context of a human being's life, and when it does, something not unlike the Buddhist Nirvana—something transcendent and inexplicable—occurs: "[W]hat remains after the complete abolition of the will is, for all who are still full of the will, assuredly nothing. But also conversely, to those in whom the will has turned and denied itself, this very real world of ours with all its suns and galaxies, is—nothing."[7]

There is a point to human existence, according to Schopenhauer. True, the will is aimless. And true, "existence is certainly to be regarded as an error or mistake."[8] But there is a point, or an aim, of our existence, and as Schopenhauer characteristically words it, it seems to be a trivial, negative point or aim: "[N]othing else can be stated as the aim of our existence except the knowledge that it would be better for us not to exist. This . . . is the most important of all truths."[9] If indeed this is "the most important of all truths," then we should, perhaps, analyze it carefully. The "aim of our existence" is "knowledge"—knowledge of a particular type. Our task in life is to acquire the knowledge that would enable us to conclude "that it would be better for us not to exist." What kind of knowledge would enable us

7. *WWR*-1, 411–12.   8. *WWR*-2, 605.
9. *WWR*-2, 605.

to draw that strange conclusion? The knowledge that the will to live, our very being-in-itself, is "involved in a delusion."[10] But, of course, it cannot stop there. That kind of knowledge might lead to some sort of doctrine of ethical suicide, and Schopenhauer condemns suicide.[11] It is, rather, knowledge such that the will itself can freely recognize the delusion in which it is involved, and can freely choose to abolish itself. It is not an abstract, reasoned-to kind of knowledge; it is intuitive and finds its expression in experience.[12]

It must be admitted that at this point Schopenhauer leaves conventional Western philosophical concepts behind, and that fact has caused some commentators, like the prolific Schopenhauer scholar Bryan Magee, to reject his doctrine of the denial of the will to live almost out of hand.[13] Magee, although arguing that Schopenhauer's doctrine of the denial of the will to live is a serious flaw in his system, took pains to minimize the "flaw": "But the work of every great philosopher has severe shortcomings. What makes such work great is not the absence of great faults but the presence of great insights."[14]

One of Magee's objections to the doctrine of the denial of the will to live is that Schopenhauer, as we shall see and examine later, denies the existence of freedom of the will in individual human beings. The only "will" that possesses freedom is the will as thing-in-itself. Magee's objection on this ground can be questioned. Recall that, for Schopenhauer, it is not the individual human being who denies the will to live, but rather it is the *will* itself that denies *itself*, and chooses to become quiescent and cease its aimless striving. True, the denial occurs in the context of the life of the individual, and that may

---

10. *WWR*-2, 606.

11. But see *Parerga*, vol. 2, ch. 13, 306–11, where Schopenhauer discounts all but one of the moral arguments against suicide. "The only valid moral reason against suicide . . . lies in the fact that suicide is opposed to the attainment of the highest moral goal since it substitutes for the real salvation from this world of woe and misery one that is merely apparent." *Parerga*, vol. 2, ch. 13, 309.

12. *WWR*-1, 304.   13. Magee, 242–43.

14. Magee, 243.

be a bit wanting in elucidation, but the denial event does not violate Schopenhauer's assertion that the individual has no true freedom of will.

Magee's second objection is that Schopenhauer clearly makes the mind subservient to the will throughout his philosophy, and this is a stronger objection. Schopenhauer does indeed make the will superior to the mind, and his doctrine of the denial of the will seems to allow that the individual mind or the acquired knowledge of the individual is what informs the will as thing in itself of the futility of its feeding on itself, and thus forms the occasion of the will as thing in itself, again in the context of the life of that individual, choosing to deny itself. One answer to the objection may be that, by implication, Schopenhauer is simply declaring that the will is superior to the mind, except that in this one unique instance, that is, the will as thing-in-itself seeing itself as it really is, the mind does inform the will. Even then, it informs the will as thing-in-itself without controlling its choice. The will as thing-in-itself can still choose to continue to *affirm* itself, to continue to sink its teeth into its own flesh, as it were. The uniqueness of this one instance of choosing led by information will be seen later in the material on Schopenhauer and Luther.

In his doctrine of the denial of the will to live, Schopenhauer has indeed left Western philosophical concepts far behind. Up until now, he has been expressing himself as a philosopher, using the vocabulary and the methodology of philosophy. But how to describe a nonabstract nonreasoned-to kind of knowledge in the vocabulary and methodology of philosophy? Here Schopenhauer calls upon myth and symbol:[15]

---

15. The importance of myth and symbol to psychology and metaphysics has since been widely recognized, especially in the writings of Carl Jung. See, e.g., Carl G. Jung, *Symbols of Transformation* (2nd ed., trans. R. F. C. Hull [Princeton, N.J.: Princeton University Press, 1967]); and *The Archetypes and the Collective Unconscious*

> [T]hat great fundamental truth contained in Christianity as well as in Brahmanism and Buddhism, the need for salvation from an existence given up to suffering and death, and its attainability through the denial of the will, hence by a decided opposition to nature, is beyond all comparison the most important truth there can be.
>
> ...
>
> But in order to understand the truth itself contained in this myth, we must regard human beings not merely in time as entities independent of one another, but must comprehend the (Platonic) Idea of man. . . . Now if we keep in view the Idea of man, we see that the Fall of Adam represents man's finite, animal, sinful nature, in respect of which he is just a being abandoned to limitation, sin, suffering, and death. On the other hand, the conduct, teaching, and death of Jesus Christ represent the eternal, supernatural side, the freedom, the salvation of man. Now, as such and *potentiâ*, every person is Adam as well as Jesus, according as he comprehends himself, and his will thereupon determines him.[16]

It is startling when we read Schopenhauer's statement "every person *is* Adam as well as Jesus." But if time, space, causality, plurality, and individuation are mere impositions of the structure of the perceiving mind, and are not attributes of true reality (and this is precisely the

---

(2nd ed., trans. R. F. C. Hull [Princeton, N.J.: Princeton University Press, 1968]); Carl G. Jung and Carl Kerenyi, *Essays on a Science of Mythology*, trans. R. F. C. Hull (Princeton, N.J.: Princeton University Press, 1949); and James N. Powell, *The Tao of Symbols* (New York: Quill, 1982). Jung himself was strongly influenced by the writings of Schopenhauer. See Carl G. Jung, *Memories, Dreams, Reflections*, trans. R. and C. Winston (New York: Random House, 1963), 69–72. Both Jung and Schopenhauer saw Jesus Christ as the symbol or embodiment or personification of the goal of human existence; for Jung, the "Self" archetype; for Schopenhauer, the denial of the will to live. See Carl G. Jung, *Memories, Dreams, Reflections*, 279; and *WWR*-1, 405.

16. *WWR*-2, 628.

claim of Schopenhauer's entire metaphysical theory), then most certainly every individual is, at that deep level of true reality, every other individual. There is an identity between Adam and each of us, between Jesus and each of us, and between Jesus and Adam. Not incidentally, Saint Paul in his Epistles to the Christians at Rome and at Corinth recognized the strong, albeit contrasting, connection between the phenomenon of Jesus and the phenomenon of Adam:

> But death reigned from Adam unto Moses, even over them also who have not sinned, after the similitude of the transgression of *Adam, who is a figure of him who was to come* [i.e., Jesus]. But not as the offence, so also the gift. For if by the offence of one many died; much more the grace of God, and the gift, by the grace of one man, *Jesus Christ,* hath abounded unto many.
> . . .
> The first man Adam was made into a living soul; the last Adam [i.e., Jesus] into a quickening spirit. . . . The first man [i.e., Adam] was of the earth, earthly; the second man [i.e., Jesus] from heaven, heavenly.[17]

Somewhat parenthetically—thinking back to the Introduction, if what Schopenhauer says here possesses validity, the cat that was frolicking outside Schopenhauer's window in 1844 *was indeed* the same cat that frolicked there three centuries earlier. Perhaps not surprisingly, renowned quantum physicist Erwin Schrödinger, the original author of the cat-in-the-box quantum physics dilemma, would likely agree. Writing of the "self" in his philosophical treatise, Schrödinger opined:

---

17. Romans 5:14–15; 1 Corinthians 15:45, 47 (Douay-Rheims) (emphasis added).

> [T]he Self is not so much *linked* with what happened to its ancestors, it is not so much the product, and merely the product, of all that, but rather, in the strictest sense of the word, the SAME THING as all that: the strict, direct continuation of it, just as the Self aged fifty is the continuation of the Self aged forty.[18]

Schrödinger was well acquainted with Schopenhauer's philosophy, and held a somewhat ambivalent opinion of Schopenhauer's works: "I would [Schrödinger would] prefer personal contact with Sancho Panza rather than with Schopenhauer; he was the more decent of the two. But Schopenhauer's books are still beautiful—except when some superstitious madness suddenly breaks out in them."[19]

The source of the startling nature of Schopenhauer's comment that "every person is Adam as well as Jesus," therefore, lies not in its being inconsistent with anything Schopenhauer had said previously (it is quite consistent), but rather in its implications. If true, Schopenhauer's statement at once solves two great theological enigmas: the doctrine of the inherited responsibility for original sin and the doctrine of the mystical body of Christ. Anyone raised in the Christian tradition will recall the difficulties that theologians have had in explaining how it is that each of us is saddled with the responsibility for the original sin of Adam, difficulties so obvious that they moved the monk Pelagius in the 4th century to deny the doctrine and to found a heresy that was still being addressed a thousand years later at the Council of Trent.[20] In Schopenhauer's thought, each of us *is* Adam, and the justice of holding each of us responsible for Adam's sin exists at the level of what Schopenhauer refers to as "eternal justice."[21] At

---

18. Schrödinger, 28 (emphasis in original).
19. Schrödinger, 110.
20. See John Hardon, S.J., *The Catholic Catechism: A Contemporary Catechism of the Teachings of the Catholic Church* (Collegeville, Minn.: Liturgical Press, 1975), 99.
21. See discussion on Schopenhauer and Gandhi, supra. Also, for Schopenhauer's treatment of Adam, original sin, and the Savior, see *WWR*-1, 405–6.

the level of deep reality, we are more than our brother's keeper—we *are* our brother and sister. We *are* our neighbor. We *are* our enemy.

Schopenhauer, indeed, startles and unnerves us—not so much because he *attacks* what Christians believe, as because he somehow seems to *defend* it so much better than they have been able to defend it. The clarity with which much (though obviously not all) of Schopenhauer's thought fits the Christian mold has alarmed Schopenhauer biographer Frederick Copleston, S.J., who felt it necessary to admonish his Christian readers, through several pages of his monograph on Schopenhauer, that the philosopher should not be read as a Christian apologist.[22]

Readers, especially readers who are familiar with Nietzsche's virulent hatred of Christianity, are usually nonplussed when they come across passages in Schopenhauer's writings that are unabashedly favorable toward Christianity. Schopenhauer scholar Christopher Janaway expressed it well:

> Perhaps surprisingly, . . . when Schopenhauer turns his mind to the optimism-pessimism issue in so many words, he constantly takes his own view to coincide with the ethical core of Christianity proper, read as ascetic resignation or self-denial in the face of a world that contains only suffering.[23]

But—returning to the topic at hand—this metaphysical interidentity among us all is just that—that is, metaphysical. It exists only at the deep level of true reality, a level that is all but foreclosed from us. We must of necessity—a necessity imposed by the very structure of our perceiving minds—function at the level of phenomena, within the constraints of time, space, causality, plurality, and individuation, behind the veil of *Maya*. But there are occasional breakthroughs. At

---

22. Copleston, 209–12.
23. Christopher Janaway, ed., *The Cambridge Companion to Schopenhauer* (Cambridge: Cambridge University Press, 1999), 320.

times, the breeze of the Platonic Idea sweeps the veil aside momentarily and, as the subject of willing falls from view in the experience of a loss of sense of self in the object, we get a glimpse, as it were, of the unity of subject and object in aesthetics. Also, at times, in our relations with one another, we have another glimpse of the deep level of true reality. Aesthetics is often linked with ethics, and the two are not unconnected in Schopenhauer's thought. Just as, in aesthetics, one can reach the level of the Platonic Idea and experience the falling from view of the subject of willing and glimpse as it were the delusion of the separation of subject and object, so too, in ethics, one can also see through the delusion of plurality. The vehicle? Compassion.

Compassion

Schopenhauer identified compassion as "the sole non-egoistic motive" and "also the only genuinely moral one."[24] In doing so, he was not breaking new ground. Rousseau, in *Emile*, his great essay on education, had identified "pity and compassion" as "the sole natural virtue" and the source of all the natural virtues.[25] Moreover, Rousseau, like Schopenhauer decades later, saw an interidentification between the observer and the sufferer as defining the concept of compassion.[26]

Where Schopenhauer did break new ground was in providing a metaphysical foundation for the virtue of compassion, and for its being the original fountainhead virtue. And this is no mean feat. Immanuel Kant has been criticized for painting himself into a meta-

---

24. *Morality*, 167.
25. Jean Jacques Rousseau, *Emile*, trans. Barbara Foxley (London: J. M. Dent, 1993), 92, 94 (hereinafter, Rousseau).
26. Rousseau, 94. Schopenhauer credits Rousseau with these insights in *On the Basis of Morality*. *Morality*, 185–86.

physical corner with his conclusion that true reality, the thing-in-itself, is absolutely unknowable, thus depriving his theory of morals of the possibility of a grounding in true reality. Kant attempted to avoid the predicament by elevating "reason" in his theory of morality even above "understanding." He clearly recognized the dilemma when he observed that "understanding . . . cannot produce by its activity any other concepts than those which serve to bring the sensuous conceptions under rules, and thereby to unite them in one consciousness."[27] With "reason" at the helm ("all moral concepts have their seat and origin entirely a priori in reason"[28]), Kant's theory of morality sailed neatly into the area of "duty" and the famed categorical imperative: Act as though the maxim of your action were by your will to become a universal law of nature."[29]

We have seen that Schopenhauer wholeheartedly accepted Kant's metaphysical premises-that is, the subjectivity or ideality of space, time, and causality—but believed that he had found a way of avoiding Kant's metaphysical conclusion. Schopenhauer believed that the human being can come to a knowledge of true reality, the thing-in-itself, which he identified as "will." Thus Schopenhauer was able to tread on metaphysical ground, which Kant had to avoid. Kant was forced by his metaphysical presuppositions and conclusions to stay at the level of the intellect, which led him inexorably to the scholastic notion of reason binding will through duty. Schopenhauer had a freer hand. He could search for the source of morality not only in the intellect, but also in the "thing-in-itself." While Kant's theory of morality had to be a theory of "duty," Schopenhauer's could be (and was) a theory of "virtue."

27. Immanuel Kant, *Foundations of the Metaphysics of Morals* (1785), trans. L. Beck (Indianapolis: Bobbs-Merrill, 1959), 70–71 (hereinafter, Kant, *Foundations*).
28. Kant, *Foundations*, 28.
29. Kant, *Foundations*, 39.

Chapter 13

Schopenhauer and Quietism

Schopenhauer himself gave us a brief but keenly focused definition of "Quietism," and in doing so, connected it with the concepts of asceticism and mysticism:

> Quietism, i.e., the giving up of all willing, asceticism, i.e., intentional mortification of one's own will, and mysticism, i.e., consciousness of the identity of one's own inner being with that of all things, or with the kernel of the world, stand in the closest connexion, so that whoever professes one of them is gradually led to the acceptance of the others, even against his intention.... [T]he writers who express those teachings ... generally do not know one another; in fact, the Indian, Christian, and Mohammedan mystics, quietists, and ascetics are different in every respect except in the inner meaning and spirit of their teachings.[1]

1. *WWR*-2, 613.

Schopenhauer's point is a strong one. The giving up of all willing, the mortification of one's own individuated version of the will, and the consciousness of the identity of one's own inner being, that is, one's "will," with the inner being, that is, "will," of all things, or with "the kernel of the world," that is, the world as "will," *is* his doctrine of the denial of the will to live. And it is also the common discovery and heritage of the deepest thinkers among the world's widely divergent religious traditions, in a sense, the kernel that lies beneath all genuine religious thought.[2]

Schopenhauer's awkwardly and perhaps unfortunately named doctrine of the denial of the will to live is, in that sense, an endorsement of the great mystical understandings, Eastern and Western, that have generated the strangely divergent and yet at the same time common religious doctrines of salvation or deliverance. It is in truth more a doctrine of deliverance than of salvation—deliverance from the sufferings caused by the affirmations of the will to live that accompany daily living. In terms of Western theological understandings of the doctrine of salvation or deliverance, Schopenhauer allied himself formally and expressly with a seventeenth-century movement in Christian mystical theology called Quietism, and with an even earlier precursor of that movement, exemplified in a fourteenth-century work known as the *Theologia Germanica*. He justified his invocation of that form of Christian mystical theology by likening its tenets to those of the Eastern, predominantly Buddhist

---

2. *The Catholic Encyclopedia*, in an article understandably treating Quietism somewhat negatively, lists its presence in the "essential" features of Brahmanism and Buddhism, and also lists the Quietist tendency within Stoicism, Neoplatonism, Gnosticism, Messalianism, and Hesychiasm. The article treats some of the Catholic Christian Quietists, e.g., François Fénelon, semi-negatively by referring to their tenets as "Semiquietism." *The Catholic Encyclopedia* (Robert Appleton Company, 1911), s.v. "Quietism." The 1911 edition of *The Catholic Encyclopedia* is much more thorough than newer editions in its treatment of topics of interest to medievalists and historians of religion.

variety: "[N]ot only the religions of the East, but also true Christianity has throughout this fundamental ascetic character that my philosophy explains as denial of the will-to-live, although Protestantism, especially in its present-day form, tries to keep this dark."[3]

Schopenhauer may have regarded Quietist spirituality as *true* Christianity, but the Catholic Church did *not*. In 1687, Pope Innocent XI, after an investigation by the Holy Inquisition, issued an Apostolic Constitution[4] condemning the Quietist teachings of the Spanish Catholic priest, Miguel de Molinos, and ordering the imprisonment of the priest himself. Molinos was one of those whom Schopenhauer cited as an exemplar of the doctrine of the denial of the will to live.[5] Among the forty-three propositions taught by Molinos and condemned by the Pope were several with which Schopenhauer would have heartily agreed. For example:

1. It is necessary that man reduce his own powers to *nothingness*, and this is the interior way.

. . .

7. A soul ought to consider *neither the reward nor punishment, nor paradise, nor hell, nor death, nor eternity*.

. . .

30. Everything *sensible* which we experience in the spiritual life, is abominable, base, and unclean.[6]

Many of the other propositions are ones with which Schopenhauer would likely have agreed had he not been an atheist. For example:

12. He who gives his own free will to God should care about *nothing, neither about hell, nor about heaven;* neither ought he to

---

3. *WWR*-2, 615.
4. Pope Innocent XI, *Coelestis Pastor* (November 20, 1687).
5. *WWR*-2, 614–15.
6. Pope Innocent XI (emphasis added).

have a desire for his own perfection, nor for virtues, nor his own sanctity, nor his own salvation—the hope of which he ought to remove.[7]

Schopenhauer's reliance on the Christian Quietist mystics is extensive, both quantitatively and qualitatively. In volume 1, the 1819 edition of *The World as Will and Representation,* Schopenhauer cites the following Christian Quietist thinkers: Jeanne-Marie Bouvier de la Mothe Guyon (commonly known as Madame Guyon), François Fénelon (Guyon's confessor), the anonymous author of the *Theologia Germanica,* Meister Eckhart, and Joannes Tauler.[8] In volume 2, the 1844 edition, he added citations to Molinos and Mother Ann Lee, who founded the Millennial Church or United Society of Believers, a Christian Quietist sect more commonly known as the Shakers.[9]

Madame Guyon (1648–1717) was a seventeenth-century Catholic who wrote and taught a Quietist form of Catholic piety and who was imprisoned and persecuted by Church authorities for her efforts. François Fénelon (1651–1715) was a Catholic priest and a contemporary and friend of Madame Guyon. He too was persecuted by Church authorities, but escaped harsher punishments by an act of submission to the authority of the Church, involving an agreement not to publish a planned Quietist book. Needless to say, although the writings of Madame Guyon and François Fénelon are highly praised in some Christian circles, they are not looked upon with favor within *Catholic* Christian circles.[10]

The anonymous author of the *Theologia Germanica* (ca. 1350), Meister Eckhart (1260–1328), and Joannes Tauler (1300–61) were all

7. Pope Innocent XI (emphasis added).
8. *WWR*-1, 381–91.
9. *WWR*-2, 614, 626.
10. See, e.g., Ronald A. Knox, *Enthusiasm: A Chapter in the History of Religion* (Oxford: Oxford University Press, 1950; Notre Dame, Ind.: University of Notre Dame Press, 1994), 231–355 (hereinafter, Knox).

fourteenth-century figures in the history of Christianity. Certainly they can be classified as Quietist mystical theologians, although the name "Quietist" did not attach itself to the movement until the time of Miguel de Molinos in the seventeenth century.

The origins of Quietist spirituality in Christian theology hark back to the many biblical passages that advocate self-denial. For example: "Then Jesus said to his disciples: If any man will come after me, let him *deny himself* and *take up his cross* and follow me. For he that will save his life shall lose it; and he that shall lose his life for my sake shall find it."[11] The text of his magnum opus reveals that Schopenhauer, atheist though he was, was well acquainted with the biblical passages that suggest a Quietist spirituality:

> We find commanded by the Apostles [Schopenhauer wrote] love for our neighbor as for ourselves, returning of hatred with love and good actions. Patience, meekness, endurance of all possible affronts and injuries without resistance, moderation in eating and drinking for suppressing desire, resistance to the sexual impulse, even complete if possible for us. Here we see the first stages of asceticism or of real denial of the will; this last expression [i.e., denial of the will (or will to live)] denotes what is called in the Gospels denying the self and taking of the cross upon oneself.[12]

In this regard, Schopenhauer stated that "we might ... regard the New Testament as the first initiation [into the denial of the will to live], the mystics as the second."[13] The mystics to whom he referred were the great Christian mystics of the fourteenth, sixteenth and

---

11. Matthew 16:24–25 (Douay-Rheims). Schopenhauer himself cited these verses and also Mark 8:34–35, and Luke 9:23–24 and 14:26–27, 33. *WWR*-1, 386.

12. *WWR*-1, 386. Schopenhauer cited, in connection with these statements, *Matthew* 16:24–25, Mark 8:34–35, and Luke 9:23–24 and 14 26–27 and 33.

13. *WWR*-1, 387.

seventeenth centuries. Named expressly in the context of the above-quoted statement are François Fénelon, the anonymous author of the *Theologia Germanica*, Meister Eckhart, and Joannes Tauler.[14]

Historically, a mystical theology of self-denial dates to the near beginnings of Christianity. Dionysius the Areopagite (also known as "Pseudo-Dionysius") in the fourth century A.D., proclaimed:

> Let this be my prayer; ... in the diligent exercise of mystical contemplation, leave behind the senses and the operations of the intellect, and all things sensible and intellectual, and all things in the world of being and nonbeing, that you may arise by unknowing towards the union, as far as is attainable, with it that transcends all being and knowledge. For by the unceasing and absolute renunciation of yourself and of all things you may be borne on high, through pure and entire self-abnegation into the superessential Radiance of the Divine Darkness.[15]

It was with the author of the *Theologia Germanica*, however, that Quietist spirituality began to coalesce, in the fourteenth century, with what would later become Schopenhauer's doctrine of the denial of the will to live. The author of the *Theologia Germanica* is unknown, and in the work, the author merely identified himself as "a friend of [God] ... once a German knight, a priest and a warden in the German house in Frankfurt."[16] The appellation "friend of God" was probably not simply descriptive of the anonymous author's de-

---

14. *WWR*-1, 387.

15. Dionysius the Areopagite, *The Mystical Theology*, reproduced in *Pseudo Dionysius: The Complete Works*, trans. Colm Luibheid (Mahwah, N.J.: Paulist Press, 1987), 135. Schopenhauer himself cites another work of Dionysius the Areopagite, the *De Divinis Nominibus* (On the divine names), approvingly. See *WWR*-2, 86.

16. *The Theologia Germanica of Martin Luther*, trans. Bengt Hoffman, Classics of Western Spirituality (Mahwah, N.J. Paulist Press, 1980), 55 (hereinafter, *Theologia Germanica* (Luther ed.). Despite this awkwardly named version of the *Theologia Germanica*, Martin Luther was not its author. It is a fourteenth-century work, and Luther is credited with rediscovering it in the sixteenth century. Interestingly,

votional attitude towards God. There was, in the thirteenth and fourteenth centuries a formal Christian movement called the "Friends of God" whose members taught "renunciation of self, the ongoing revelation of God through the work of the Holy Spirit in man, and the ultimate union between God and man."[17] The *Theologia Germanica* was likely written about 1350, and Schopenhauer had this to say about the work: "The precepts and doctrines given in it [i.e., in the *Theologia Germanica*] are the most perfect explanation, springing from deep inward conviction, of what I have described as the denial of the will-to-live."[18]

It is easy to find many of the underpinnings of Schopenhauer's doctrine of the denial of the will to live in the *Theologia Germanica*, but only if one is willing to gainsay the anonymous author's theism and Schopenhauer's atheism. The Wuerzburg edition of the *Theologia Germanica* begins with a prescription for one who desires to be perfect, and its prescription is quite fairly describable as an analogue to Schopenhauer's understanding of the denial of the will to live:

> [I]n whatsoever creature the Perfect shall be known, therein creature-nature, qualities, the I, the Self and the like, must all be lost and done away. This is the meaning of that saying of Saint Paul: "When that which is perfect is come" (that is, when it is known), "then that which is in part"[19] (to wit, creature-na-

---

the text discovered by Luther is *not* the text preferred by Schopenhauer. In 1851, a so-called Wuerzburg (although Schopenhauer calls it the Stuttgart) edition of the text of the *Theologia Germanica* was discovered, which Schopenhauer preferred as being far less adulterated than the Luther text. See *WWR*-1 387. The 1851 text is still available: *Theologia Germanica*, trans. Susanna Winkworth (London: Macmillan, 1893) (hereinafter, *Theologia Germanica*). It is also available in a revised version: *Theologia Germanica*, trans. Susanna Winkworth, ed. Joseph Bernhart (New York: Pantheon, 1949). The 1851 text self-describes the author as "[God's] friend, who aforetime was of the Teutonic order in Frankfort."

17. *Theologia Germanica* (Luther ed.), 7.
18. *WWR*-1, 387.
19. The quotation is from 1 Corinthians 13:10: "But when that which is perfect is come, that which is in part shall be done away." (Douay-Rheims).

ture, qualities, the I, the Self, the Mine) will be despised and counted for naught.[20]

Schopenhauer's own definition of "Quietism," that is, "the giving up of all willing," can be seen in the above passage from the *Theologia Germanica:* The "I, the Self, the Mine" must be "despised and counted for naught." Schopenhauer's definition of "mysticism," however, that is, "consciousness of the identity of one's own inner being with that of all things, or with the kernel of the world," is a bit more problematic. There are hints of this interidentity in the *Theologia Germanica*, as when the anonymous author makes the following remarkably Schopenhauerian (despite the theistic base) statement: "There is an Eternal Will, which is in God a first Principle and substance, apart from all works and effects, and the same will is in Man, or the creature. . . . [T]he will in the creature, which we call a created will, is as truly God's as the Eternal Will, and is not of the creature."[21]

It must, however, be acknowledged that whereas Schopenhauer finds the bliss of desirelessness in his own version of Quietism, arguably making his version much more akin to Eastern mysticism's doctrine of Nirvana, the author of the *Theologia Germanica* finds love in his version of Quietism, specifically the undistracted and pure love of God: "And as God and the True Light are without all self-will, selfishness, and self-seeking, so do the I, the Me, the Mine, and the like, belong unto the natural and false Light."[22] Schopenhau-

---

20. *Theologia Germanica*, 5; chapter 1. The Luther edition words it this way: "[I]n whichever creature this perfect life is to be known, creatureliness, createdness, selfishness, must be abandoned and destroyed.

"This is what Saint Paul's words mean when he writes that when the Perfect comes—that is when it is known in the heart—then that which only exists in part—creatureliness, createdness, selfishness, impulse-ridden desire—will be spurned and considered naught."

Theologia Germanica (Luther ed.), 61.

21. *Theologia Germanica*, 197, chap. 51.

22. *Theologia Germanica*, 143, chap. 40. The *Theologia Germanica* (Luther ed.) version of this passage is found at pp. 122–23.

er himself actually quoted the above passage and followed it with an appeal to what might be referred to as less theistic authorities:

> In keeping with this [i.e., the quote from the *Theologia Germanica*], it says in the *Kural,* translated from the Tamil by Graul, p. 8: "The passion of the mind directed outwards and that of the I inwards cease" (cf. verse 346). And in the *Manual of Buddhism* by Spence Hardy, p. 258, the Buddha says: "My disciples reject the idea that I am this or this is mine."[23]

There is, in Schopenhauer's magnum opus a lengthy discourse on what he regards as true Christianity, replete with scriptural quotations and accounts of Church history,[24] the summation of which is worth reproducing:

> [T]hat great fundamental truth contained in Christianity as well as in Brahmanism and Buddhism, the need for salvation from an existence given up to suffering and death, and its attainability through the denial of the will, hence by a decided opposition to nature, is beyond all comparison the most important truth there can be.[25]

In the first volume of his magnum opus, Schopenhauer made the same statement in a different, more particularized form, relating his teachings to the traditional Christian doctrines of original sin and salvation, and invoking Jesus Christ no less as the paragon of those teachings:

> The doctrine of original sin (affirmation of the will) and of salvation (denial of the will) is really the great truth which constitutes the kernel of Christianity. . . . Accordingly, we should inter-

---

23. *WWR*-2, 613–14.   24. *WWR*-2, 615–33.
25. *WWR*-2, 628.

pret Jesus Christ always in the universal, as the symbol or personification of the denial of the will-to-live....²⁶

The great Jesuit historian of philosophy Frederick Copleston has seen, as the final denouement of Schopenhauer's doctrine of the denial of the will to live, not the heavenly bliss of the Christian mystics whom he so frequently cited, but rather "complete extinction, the abyss of nothingness."²⁷ Schopenhauer, however, anticipated Copleston's conclusion:

> I do not wish ... to conceal an objection concerning the last part of the discussion [Schopenhauer wrote].... The objection is that, after our observations have finally brought us to the point where we have before our eyes in perfect saintliness the denial and surrender of all willing, and thus a deliverance from a world whose whole existence presented itself to us as suffering, this now appears to us as a transition into empty *nothingness*.²⁸

Schopenhauer's answer to this objection is cryptic and, at the same time, challenging. In a sense, Schopenhauer accepts the nothingness: "We must not ... evade it [i.e., the nothingness], as the Indians do, by myths and meaningless words, such as reabsorption in *Brahman* or the *Nirvana* of the Buddhists."²⁹ But the nothingness that Schopenhauer accepts is, he points out, not likely to be anything like the nothingness envisioned by his critics. It quite simply has no referents. It cannot be the emptiness that usually comes to mind when we try to think about nothingness or extinction, that is, something like empty space with nothing occupying it. Recall that, in Schopen-

---

26. *WWR*-1, 405.
27. Copleston, 189 (1946).
28. *WWR*-1 408–9 (emphasis in original).
29. *WWR*-1, 411.

hauer's theory, both time and space are simply impositions of our organ of perception. When willing ceases, time and space also go out of existence. A timeless and spaceless nothingness is, it may be fair to say, impossible to envision. In the end, upon rejecting the Hindu concept of reabsorption in *Brahman* and the Buddhist *Nirvana*, Schopenhauer was left with the "nothingness" experienced by the Christian mystics, as he writes of

> those who have overcome the world, in whom the will, having reached complete self-knowledge, has found itself again in everything, and then freely denied itself, and who then merely wait to see the last trace of the will vanish with the body that is animated by that trace. Then, instead of the restless pressure and effort; instead of the constant transition from desire to apprehension and from joy to sorrow; instead of the never-satisfied and never-dying hope that constitutes the life-dream of the man who wills, we see that peace that is higher than all reason, that ocean-like calmness of the spirit, that deep tranquillity, that unshakeable confidence and serenity, whose mere reflection in the countenance . . . is a complete and certain gospel.[30]

Schopenhauer ends his treatment of the "nothingness" objection with a thought that seems more like a challenge than a surrender:

> We freely acknowledge that what remains after the complete abolition of the will is, for all who are still full of the will, assuredly nothing. But also conversely, to those in whom the will has turned and denied itself, this very real world of ours with all its suns and galaxies, is—nothing.[31]

30. *WWR*-1, 411.
31. *WWR*-1, 411–12.

At one point, the author of the *Theologia Germanica* stated what might be a fair analogy of sorts to Schopenhauer's doctrine of the denial of the will to live, albeit in theistic, Christian terms. In the following passage (using the text discovered by Luther) the analogy may emerge if we substitute Schopenhauer's will for the divine appellations:

> Not a few argue that man before God [for Schopenhauer, will] should become free from rules, will, love, knowledge, and so on. However, this cannot mean that there is no knowledge in man.... No, this way of talking ... actually means that acknowledging God [for Schopenhauer, will] becomes so clear and perfect that this knowledge is not man's knowledge or any creature's knowledge but the knowledge of the Eternal [for Schopenhauer, the eternal will], which is to say the Eternal Word [for Schopenhauer, the eternal will]. And thus man—or the creature—sets out on a new quest, claiming nothing for his own self. The less he assumes on his own behalf the more perfect and whole he becomes.

The same text from the version preferred by Schopenhauer himself reads:

> Certain men say that we ought to be without will, wisdom, love, desire, knowledge, and the like. Hereby is not to be understood that there is to be no knowledge in man.... But it meaneth that man's knowledge should be so clear and perfect that he should acknowledge of a truth that in himself he neither hath nor can do any good thing, and that none of his knowledge, wisdom and art, his will, love and good works do come from himself, nor are of any man, nor of any creature, but that all these are of the Eternal God [for Schopenhauer, the eternal will], from whom

they all proceed. . . . [W]ith the will, and love and desire, and the like . . . the less we call these things our own, the baser and less pure and perfect do they become.[32]

Recall, however, that the only entity that has "free will" in Schopenhauer's scheme of things is the will itself, *as* thing-in-itself, that is, the will "writ large," not the phenomenon of will that appears in the individual life of the individual human being. Recall also that since the will is constantly involved in affirming itself in individual phenomena, most often at the expense of itself in other individual phenomena, the will is constantly "sinking its teeth into its own flesh." And we have seen that the alternative to this unpleasant state of affairs, according to Schopenhauer, is for the *will* to deny i*tself*—note: not for the individual human being to deny the will, but for the *will* itself to deny *itself,* to become quiescent, to cease its aimless striving. This event—the will denying itself—*can*, Schopenhauer asserts, occur in the context of a human being's life, when the human being abandons his own willing upon coming to the knowledge that he has only been participating in the will "feeding on itself" and thereupon the mind of the individual human being touches the will itself. At that point, the will itself comes upon a choice—to continue to affirm itself, or to deny itself.

So too the author of the *Theologia Germanica* sees Christian salvation in terms of the individual abandoning his own will, desire, and so on, and in coming to the insightful knowledge that all is God's, not one's own, and that insight is so clear and pure that it becomes God's Own knowledge, and union with the all-loving God occurs.

It is curious that Schopenhauer could admire so much the mysti-

---

32. See *Theologia Germanica* (Luther ed.), 64, and *Theologia Germanica*, 12–14, chap. 5.

cal theology of those whose Ultimate is an all-loving personal God, and settle for himself on an "ultimate" that was a purposeless, directionless, impersonal force. The end result of Schopenhauer's denial of the will to live and the Christian mystic's union with God is, however, similar. The individual becomes whole, more perfect. So too the initial problem for both is similar: the need to quiet the individual will and desire, to turn one's back on a world wallowing in the after-effects of Original Sin (for the Christian mystic), or on a purposeless, directionless will feeding on itself (for Schopenhauer).

It may well be that the analogy between the Christian mystic's God and Schopenhauer's will is improper and unfair. Perhaps the better analogy is between Schopenhauer's will on the one hand, and what it is that needs to be overcome (in the mind of the Christian mystic) on the other, that is, the "god of this world,"[33] namely, Satan. One Christian mystic whom Schopenhauer frequently cites is Miguel de Molinos, the seventeenth-century Spanish mystical theologian who is often regarded as the founder of Quietism. In the year after his death in 1696, Molinos's teachings were declared to be heretical by Pope Innocent XI. One of Molinos's teachings bears heavily on this idea of the proper analogy being the analogy between Schopenhauer's will and Satan: "Thou wilt never get up the Mountain of Perfection, nor to any high Throne of Peace Internal, if thou art only govern'd by *thy own* Will: This cruel and fierce Enemy of God, and of thy soul, must be conquered; thy own Direction, thy own Judgment, must be subdued and deposed as Rebels. . . ."[34] In other words, the

---

33. See 2 Corinthians 4:4, where Satan is referred to expressly as "the god of this world" (Douay-Rheims).

34. Miguel de Molinos, *The Spiritual Guide*, trans. an anonymous Quietist (written, 1678; printed at Venice, 1685; London: 1688) bk. 2, chap. ix (emphasis added). Monsignor Ronald Knox, the famed translator of the Bible into vernacular English, has rendered that same passage a bit more mellifluously: "You will never reach the mountain of perfection . . . if you are governed by *your own* will. This is

will, individuated in the individual human being, feeding on itself as individuated in other human beings, is the "cruel and fierce Enemy of God." But the will *un*individuated, enlightened if you will with the knowledge of the futility of its past endless activity of feeding upon itself, is no longer the "cruel and fierce Enemy of God" and becomes instead the means of ascending "the Mountain of Perfection" and the "high Throne of Peace Internal."

Sacred Scripture most certainly informed the teachings of Molinos and the other Quietist mystics and, despite its open allegiance to theism, Sacred Scripture was often invoked positively, if not relied upon, by Schopenhauer, most especially in his treatment of the denial of the will to live. A Scriptural analogy may, at this point, be helpful in illustrating the proper analogical fit for Schopenhauer's will in the theology of Quietism.

In the well-known creation account in the Bible, Adam and Eve's troubles (and derivatively the troubles of all of us) were occasioned by the eating, contrary to the command of God, of the fruit of a particular tree in the Garden of Eden. Everyone knows that the particular tree in question was located at the center of the Garden.[35] Many people, however, are unaware that there were *two* trees in the center of the Garden,[36] the forbidden tree, that is, the tree of knowledge of good and evil, and the tree of life. Eating the fruit of the tree of *life* was *not* forbidden,[37] and indeed may have been encouraged by God, because after and because of their sin, when Adam and Eve were cast out of the Garden, God stationed an angel with a flaming sword at the entrance to the Garden so that Adam and Eve would *not* have access to the tree of life.[38] And so it was that, instead of eating of the

---

the cruel beast, God's and your soul's enemy, which you have to conquer...." Knox, 239 (emphasis added).

35. Genesis 2:9 and 3:3.   36. Genesis 2:9.
37. Genesis 2:16–17.   38. Genesis 3:24.

fruit of *that* tree, as was originally intended, Eve, and then Adam, ate of the fruit of the tree of knowledge of good and evil.

What, one may ask, is wrong with acquiring a knowledge of good and evil? Perhaps surprisingly, an answer to that question comes rather easily from the philosophy of Schopenhauer (*via* Kant) and from the findings of modern physics. Adam and Eve (and indeed all of us) exist in *time*. In Schopenhauer's and Kant's philosophies, "time" is merely an imposition of the individual's organ of perception, a precondition of the ability to process the input of information about reality. In the findings of modern physics, "time" is merely a dimension, an inseparable ingredient in "space-time." God exists in *eternity*. We exist, and process knowledge, in *time*. To put it simply, only God has "the Big Picture." We can only see the probable immediate consequences of our actions. We know good, and we know evil, but we do not have God's vantage point, outside of time. We have, in other words, a knowledge of good and evil, but not the wisdom needed to handle that knowledge. Hence it is that we constantly settle for the small "g" good instead of the capital "G" Good. To put this theistic analogy into the context of Schopenhauer's philosophy, *affirming* the will to live may be seen as, in a sense, a "good"—at least a natural good. But lacking the wisdom to handle that "good," we constantly find ourselves in Schopenhauer's dilemma. In pure Schopenhauerian terms, however, good and evil are defined always in relation to the will. In Schopenhauerian pessimism, "good" is likely never "good" but rather evil.

The end result of both the theistic analogy to Schopenhauer's view and of Schopenhauer's own view itself is, however, the same. Our individuated "will" affirms itself by sinking its teeth into itself, that is, into the individuated "wills" of other creatures. Mixing the Schopenhauerian with the Christian, we find that *affirming* the will to live is serving "the cruel and fierce Enemy of God," and *denying* the will to live (the salvation event in Schopenhauer's thought) reopens the gates to the Garden of Eden and once again gives access to the tree of life.[39]

All this is by way of advancing the argument that Schopenhauer's doctrine of the denial of the will to live is not completely equivalent to the Hindu *Brahman* or the Buddhist *Nirvana*—at least not equivalent to understandings of *Brahman* or *Nirvana* that contemplate an absolute extinction. True, Schopenhauer uses the word "nothingness" to describe the situation following the denial of the will to live, but so too do both the Christian Quietist mystics and even the more orthodox contemporary Christian mystical theologians. For example, one contemporary Catholic theologian and law professor emeritus, Father David Granfield, O.S.B., writes of the individual's own "nothingness," of God Himself being "no thing," and finally and most relevantly to the subject at hand, of "the *positive nothingness that is God.*"[40] In writing that God is "no thing," Father Granfield obviously means that God transcends "thing-ness," not that God is nonexistent. Schopenhauer, who really did believe that God is nonexistent, nonetheless wrote:

> [W]e have to banish the dark impression of that nothingness, which as the final goal hovers behind all virtue and holiness, and which we fear as children fear darkness. We must not even evade it, as the Indians do, by myths and meaningless words, such as reabsorption in *Brahman,* or the *Nirvana* of the Buddhists.[41]

---

39. See Revelation (Apocalypse) 22:1–5, 14.
40. David Granfield, O.S.B., *Heightened Consciousness: The Mystical Difference* (New York: Paulist Press, 1991), 36, 90, 144. Father Granfield writes of the individual's own "nothingness" on p. 36, of God Himself being "no thing" on p. 90, and finally of "the positive nothingness that is God" on p. 144.
41. *WWR*-1, 411.

The implication is that we must confront the notion of "mystical" nothingness being nothing but fearful darkness, and in doing so we must not wallow in myth, not even in the ancient and revered myths of the Hindu and Buddhist thinkers.

For Schopenhauer, something does lie on the other side of the denial of the will to live, something close—as close as a misanthropic atheist can possibly come—to Father Granfield's "*positive* nothingness that is God" or to "the peace of God, which surpasses all understanding"[42] found by the Christian Quietist mystics. And so it was that Schopenhauer could characterize what it is that we will see on that other side of the denial of the will to live in these strongly positive and perhaps Christian-sounding terms:

> [I]nstead of the restless pressure and effort; instead of the constant transition from desire to apprehension and from joy to sorrow; instead of the never-satisfied and never-dying hope that constitutes the life-dream of the man who wills, we see *that peace that is higher than all reason,* that ocean-like calmness of the spirit, that deep tranquility, that unshakeable confidence and serenity, whose mere reflection in the countenance . . . is a complete and certain gospel.[43]

42. Philippians 4:7.
43. *WWR*-1, 411 (emphasis added).

Chapter 14

Schopenhauer and Luther

Schopenhauer's great moral insights, for example, his ethic of virtue rather than duty and his identification of compassion as "the sole non-egoistic motive" and "also the only genuinely moral one,"[1] were, in that context of morality, very much an echo of the great insight Martin Luther displayed in his *Commentary on the Epistle to the Romans*. Schopenhauer saw no good in doing something for duty's sake when the doing of the act goes against the true character of the person involved.[2] Luther had the same view:

> [W]ith human laws—the law is fulfilled by works, even though there is no heart in them. But God judges according to what is at the bottom of the heart, and for this reason, his law makes its demands on the inmost heart and cannot be satisfied with works, but rather punishes works that are done otherwise than from the bottom of the heart as hypocrisy and lies.[3]

---

1. *Morality*, 167.
2. See, e.g., *Morality*, 65–66, where Schopenhauer states Kant's duty-oriented position and calls it "absurd moral pedantry."
3. Martin Luther, *Commentary on the Epistle to the Romans* (1552), trans. J. Mueller (Grand Rapids, Mich.: Zondervan, 1954), xiii (hereinafter, Luther).

There are many parallels in the thinking of Martin Luther and Arthur Schopenhauer. Both believed that goodness or badness comes from the deep heart (Luther) or character (Schopenhauer). Both saw the flesh (Luther) or the phenomenal self (Schopenhauer) as the source of evil. Both argued against the concept of the freedom of the will. And finally both believed that change is possible only through some cataclysmic, paradoxical, and supernatural event: God's grace and the gift of faith, for Luther, and the denial of the will to live, for Schopenhauer.[4]

Schopenhauer, echoing Luther, saw the foundation of morality as a problem of metaphysics, rather than as a problem of ethics: at issue is what one *is*, rather than what one *does*.[5] And his metaphysics has something quite clear to say about the ethical milieu in which we find ourselves:

> [N]ature has her center in every individual, for each one is the entire will-to-live. Accordingly, he conceives himself as the kernel and centre of the world, and considers himself infinitely important. On the other hand, if he looks outwards, he is then in the province of the representation, of the mere phenomenon, where he sees himself as an individual among an infinite number of other individuals, and consequently as something extremely insignificant, in fact quite infinitesimal. . . . To this, therefore, is due the great difference between what each one necessarily is in his own eyes, and what he is in the eyes of others, consequently *egoism*, with which everyone reproaches everyone else.[6]

The base condition in which we find ourselves is egoism. And because our perceiving minds function normally in the world of phenomena, where time, space, causality, *plurality*, and *individuality*

---

4. See *WWR*-2, 607.   5. *Morality*, 144–45.
6. *WWR*-2, 599–600

hold sway, our egoism is conditioned by those factors. We separate the world into "I" and "Not-I." But, according to Schopenhauer's metaphysics, at that *other* level—the level of thing-in-itself or true reality—none of those factors holds sway. At the level of true reality, our egoism is a very basic and fundamental error. And it is not simply an error of *personal* illusion that besets each of us (although it is that). The *"will" itself,* since it exists whole and entire in each of us, is in error. In Schopenhauer's words, "[i]ndividuation . . . keeps the will-to-live in error as to its own true nature."[7]

We have seen that Schopenhauer does not find the gap between the world of phenomenon and the world of thing-in-itself to be unbridgeable.[8] And it is in the bridging of this metaphysical gap that Schopenhauer locates virtue (and vice).

> In some men the sight of other men at once arouses a hostile feeling, in that their innermost being declares: "Not me!" There are others in whom it at once arouses a friendly interest: "Me once more!" Countless gradations lie between these two extremes.
>
> . . .
>
> What distinguishes a moral virtue from a moral vice is whether the basic feeling towards others behind it is one of envy or one of pity: for every man bears these two diametrically opposed qualities within him, inasmuch as they arise from the comparison between his own condition and that of others which he cannot help making.[9]

---

7. *WWR*-2, 601.
8. See material on The Kantian Flaw and Schopenhauer's Own Claim to Fame, supra.
9. *Essays*, 144, 134.

It is fairly easy to see where envy and pity (compassion) come from, respectively. Envy results from the fundamental error identified in Schopenhauer's metaphysics, egoism. Compassion, on the other hand, has stronger roots. It comes from the recognition that "[m]y true inner being exists in every living thing as directly as it makes itself known in my self-consciousness only to me."[10] For Schopenhauer, "genuine virtue . . . must spring from the intuitive knowledge that recognizes in another's individuality the same inner nature as in one's own."[11]

What emerges from all this is that, in Schopenhauer's thought, there are only three fundamental "incentives" of human action. And one or another stimulates all motives. They are:

a. Egoism: this desires one's own weal (is boundless)
b. Malice: this desires another's woe (goes to the limits of extreme cruelty)
c. Compassion: this desires another's weal (goes to the length of nobleness and magnanimity)[12]

Only one of these incentives has anything to do with moral worth, namely, compassion. Compassion is "the primary ethical phenomenon."[13] It is "a state of being immediately motivated by the sufferings of another."[14] It is "simply and solely . . . the real basis of all *voluntary* justice and *genuine* lovingkindness. Only insofar as an action has sprung from compassion does it have moral value; and every action resulting from any other motives has none."[15]

Schopenhauer made it clear that the compassion that lay at the base of his system of morality had ontological significance. It was not the shallow, ephemeral feeling that some had held it to be:

10. *Morality*, 210.
11. *WWR*-1, 367–68.
12. *Morality*, 145.
13. *Morality*, 148.
14. *Morality*, 147.
15. *Morality*, 144.

> I must censure the error of Cassina. . . . His view is that compassion arises from an instantaneous deception of the imagination, since we put ourselves in the position of the sufferer, and have the idea that we are suffering *his* pains in *our* person. This is by no means the case; on the contrary, at every moment we remain clearly conscious that *he* is the sufferer, not *we;* and it is precisely in *his* person, not in ours, that we feel his pain as *his*, and do not imagine that it is ours. . . . The explanation of the possibility of this highly important phenomenon . . . can be arrived at only metaphysically.[16]

Schopenhauer was writing of a much less common phenomenon than was Cassina.[17] There are, in truth, two "compassions," one prevalent and superficial, and the other rare and ontological in depth. Tolstoy saw the difference clearly when he wrote of aristocratic women shedding tears over the performance of actors in a play while their coachmen sat shivering in the snow outside. There is a danger in recognizing that compassion is ontologically based, the danger of becoming a Francis of Assisi, a Mohandas K. Gandhi, or a Mother Teresa.[18] It is humankind's misfortune that the latter type of compassion surfaces so rarely. But its ontological base, that is, the basic unity of all existence, is present fully in each of us.

It may seem, at this point, as if Schopenhauer has laid the groundwork for a very worthwhile system of personal ethics. One may have been acting selfishly or maliciously all one's life, but with the great insight that Schopenhauer's metaphysics provides—an understanding of the fundamental unity underlying all existence—one

---

16. *Morality*, 147.
17. Ubaldo Cassina, *Saggio Analitico Sulla Compassione* (Parma: Nella Stamperia Reale, 1772).
18. Not surprisingly, Schopenhauer draws this very implication with the mention of Francis of Assisi, Gautama Buddha, and others. *WWR*-1, 384.

can change and begin to act unselfishly and altruistically and begin to grow in tolerance and love. The problem—and it is a big one—is that Schopenhauer did not believe that the human will is free in anything but a transcendental sense. Moreover, it is not that Schopenhauer's thoughts on the freedom of the human will were developed in some unconnected context, so that their application to his theory of morality might be considered accidental or problematic. He saw no way of reconciling the doctrine of free will with his theory of morality: "[I]f one assumes the freedom of the will, it is absolutely impossible to say what is the source both of virtue and of vice...."[19]

The source of virtue and vice, in Schopenhauer's thought, is "the inborn character," the "real core of the whole man."[20] And this "character" is, in Schopenhauer's thought, nothing less than the "will" itself in its particular objectification, the Platonic Idea that is represented in this or that particular human being:

> That assumption on which the necessity of the operations of all causes rests is the inner being of everything—be it merely a general natural force which manifests itself in it, or be it life force, or be it will. In every case the particular being, of whatever type, will react according to its special nature, whenever causes act upon it. This law, to which all things in the world are subject without exception, was expressed by the scholastics in the formula *operari sequitur esse*.[21]

19. *Freedom*, 56. 20. *Freedom*, 56.
21. *Freedom*, 59.

Chapter 15

On the Freedom of the Will

A very basic part of Schopenhauer's theory of justice is his treatment of the age-old issue of free will versus determinism. We saw in the introduction to this study that Schopenhauer had submitted an essay *On the Basis of Morality* to a contest sponsored by the Danish Royal Society of the Sciences, and that, although his was the only entry, he lost. There was, however, a similar essay contest in which Schopenhauer emerged as the winner. In 1839, the Scientific Society of Trondheim, Norway, awarded him the prize for his essay *On the Freedom of the Will*. It should be remembered that both essays were written two decades *after* Schopenhauer had completed the first edition of his great but then-as-yet unheralded metaphysical opus, *The World as Will and Representation*. Hence his thoughts on the freedom of the will, on the basis of morality—his theory of justice in general—flow directly from the metaphysical principles he had sought to establish.

Schopenhauer's thoughts on the freedom of the will hark back to that part of his metaphysics which deals with "Platonic Ideas." We saw earlier that for Schopenhauer the "Platonic Idea" is something quite close to the thing-in-itself, that is, "will."[1] It is, in fact, the thing-in-itself, "will," with but one limitation: it is perceived not in itself, as it really is, but rather in the relationship that object bears to perceiving subject. The "Platonic Idea," in Schopenhauer's thought, is the immediate (i.e., directly perceived) objectivity of the "will" at a definite grade.[2] The "will" does seem to reveal itself through the "Platonic Ideas" to our perceiving mind as existing at definite "grades" of objectivity: "What appears in clouds, brook, and crystal is the feeblest echo of that will which appears more completely in the plant, still more completely in man.... [T]he *essential* in all these grades of the will's objectification constitutes the *Idea*."[3]

At levels below man, Schopenhauer's "Platonic Idea" seems similar to what the scholastics would term "essence," for example, that which makes a cloud to be a cloud is its essence and that essence is shared by all other clouds. In science, the term would likely be "species." Schopenhauer eschews the term "essence" and favors "species."[4] The species in nature are the empirical correlates of the Ideas.[5]

At the level of the human being, however, Schopenhauer's understanding of "Plato's Ideas" takes a specific and most interesting turn. Each individual human being is capable of representing one special Platonic Idea: "The character of each individual man, insofar as it is thoroughly individual and not entirely included in that of the species, can be regarded as a special Idea, corresponding to a particular act of objectification of the will."[6]

Whether one accepts or rejects Schopenhauer's understanding of

1. *WWR*-1, 170.   2. *WWR*-1, 170.
3. *WWR*-1, 182.
4. See, e.g., *WWR*-1, 179 and *WWR*-2, 364–65.
5. See Hamlyn, 106.
6. *WWR*-1, 158.

"Plato's Ideas,"[7] it is clear that in positing each individual human being as a "special Idea" (in a sense, almost positing each human being as a veritable Darwinian "species" in itself), Schopenhauer was carving an enormously important place for each individual human being in his philosophy. Each human being, in Schopenhauer's thought, is a special and unique objectification of the universal "will."

With such an individualistic tinge to it, Schopenhauer's thought might be expected to move in the direction of a strong concept of individual freedom, but not so. Quite logically, and inexorably, Schopenhauer's conception of the individual human being as a special "Platonic Idea" led to the contrary conclusion. Recall that the thing-in-itself, true reality, lies outside the constraints of time, space, and causality. The thing-in-itself of each human being, what Schopenhauer refers to as each human being's *character*, is thus not determined over time. Each human being's true reality, his or her *character*, is what it is at all times, because it lies outside time. What lies *inside* time is each human being's *understanding* of his or her own character, that is, what Schopenhauer refers to as "the empirical character":[8] "[T]he empirical character . . . is . . . bound to . . . time, space, and causality. . . ."[9]

The empirical character, in the sense of a human being's *understanding* of his or her own ultimate and timeless character, can change. One can become more knowledgeable or, for that matter, less knowledgeable about one's own character, and this change produces an illusion of freedom, but it does so only by confusing "freedom," a will concept, with "knowledge," an intellect concept. It is only the knowledge and consequently the understanding that

---

7. Bryan Magee seems to consider it all but irrelevant to his (Schopenhauer's) main theses. Magee, 238–39.
8. *Freedom*, 97.
9. *Freedom*, 97.

changes. The underlying character remains what it is. The reasoning process that led Schopenhauer to conclude that there is no freedom of the will at the empirical level (the level of appearances) is not unlike the reasoning process that led some Christian theologians to adopt a doctrine of predestination.

But a certain type of freedom—yes, even freedom of the "will"—does exist in Schopenhauer's thought. Not only is a human being's thing-in-itself (or "character") not subject to time, it is also not subject to causality:

> On the other hand, the condition and basis of this whole appearance . . . is his intelligible character, i.e., his will as thing-in-itself. It is to the will in this capacity that freedom and to be sure even absolute freedom, that is, independence of the law of causality (as a mere form of appearances) properly belongs. This freedom, however, is transcendental, i.e., it does not occur in appearance. It is present only insofar as we abstract from the appearance and from all its forms in order to reach that which, since it is outside of all time, must be thought of as the inner being of man-in-himself.[10]

So, "the inner being of man-in-himself" is free. And the type of freedom that man's inner being *has* exists not in action, but rather in *being:* ". . . [W]e must no longer seek the work of our freedom in our individual actions, as the general opinion does, but in the whole being and essence *(existentia et essentia)* of the man himself."[11]

What is the significance of this "transcendental" freedom of the will—this freedom at the level of "the inner being of man-in-himself"? If freedom does exist at the deep level of true reality that

---

10. *Freedom,* 97.
11. *Freedom,* 97.

transcends time, space, and causality, how does it work? Can the inner being of man-in-himself or woman-in-herself *choose?* Choose what? To *do* this or that? No, Schopenhauer has said that we must not seek the work of freedom in individual *actions,* but rather in the individual's whole being and essence. Can the inner being of man-in-himself or woman-in-herself choose a whole new being and essence? Curiously, Martin Luther posited such an event three hundred years before Schopenhauer. Luther found it in a theological perspective, and in the context of Christian faith: "Faith . . . is a divine work in us. It changes us and make us to be born anew of God (John 1); it kills the old Adam and makes altogether different men, in heart and spirit and mind and powers, and it brings with it the Holy Ghost."[12]

Schopenhauer, of course, did not write from a theological perspective (although he often drew on those who did), but the place of this transcendental freedom of the "will" in his philosophy is no less dramatic than the place occupied by Christian salvation in Luther's theology. For Luther, it was possible for the individual human being with the grace of God through faith to "kill the old Adam." For Schopenhauer, it was possible for the individual human being, through *knowledge,* to deny the will to live. Schopenhauer does use the word "knowledge" in this context, but he also qualifies it, as though the word "knowledge" were only the closest analogue to what he has in mind:

> The *unity of that will* here alluded to, which lies beyond the phenomenon, and in which we have recognized the inner being of the phenomenal world, is a metaphysical unity. Consequently *knowledge of it is transcendent;* that is to say, it does not rest on the functions of our intellect, and is therefore not to be really grasped with them.[13]

12. Luther, xvii.
13. *WWR*-2, 323 (emphasis added).

Thus it is that two factors blunt the sharpness of Schopenhauer's position denying free will: (1) He holds that the will *is* free at the deep level of true reality, and (2) he holds that even at the level of phenomenon, where the will is not free, correction of cognition (one can, as it were, change one's opinion) can have some moral influence on one's thinking, but not on one's character, that is, not on one's inner being itself. It is only at the deep level of true reality that the will can affect one's character or true inner being. Schopenhauer's position denying free will at the level of phenomena, but admitting it at the transcendental level of true reality is not unlike that of Martin Luther. Luther denied free will, but held that the human being can, at a transcendental level (by the grace of God[14] and a trusting faith), effect a change of character to such an extent that one is a new person. In both cases, it is an all-or-nothing kind of freedom. In both cases, correction of cognition has no effect on character, the true inner being of the person, whatsoever.

> [T]he undertaking to remove the failings of character of a man by means of talk and moralizing and thus to reform his character itself, his essential morality, is exactly like the attempt to change lead into gold by external action, or by means of careful cultivation, to make an oak produce apricots.[15]

Schopenhauer and Luther also exhibited a similarity of approach when dealing with individual attempts to act in a morally good manner. There is a place for moral effort in the scheme of things. For Luther, moral effort, the effort to obey the moral law, forces the hu-

---

14. The place that "the grace of God" has in Luther's thought seems to be occupied, in Schopenhauer's thought, by the knowledge that is transcendent and that does not rest on the functions of the intellect.

15. *Freedom*, 97. Luther was, perhaps, even more vehement in denying the freedom of the will: "All testimonies (of the Scripture) which deal with Christ oppose the freedom of the will." Martin Luther, *On the Bondage of the Will*, 220, ed. Schmidt (1707).

man being to see "how deeply sin and evil are rooted in his soul."[16] The role that the moral law in the context of self-knowledge occupied in Luther's thought was occupied by correction of cognition in Schopenhauer's: "[T]hrough that which we do we only find out what we are."[17] And: "The cognitive faculty ... actually learns the nature of its own will only from its actions, empirically."[18] In both cases, "[w]e must no longer seek the work of our freedom in our individual actions, as the general opinion does, but in the whole being and essence *(existentia et essentia)* of the man himself."[19]

For Luther, this ultimate "work of freedom" is salvation by grace through faith. For Schopenhauer, it is, as we shall see, the *denial* of the will to live. For both, it amounts to surrender to (or a leap of faith in) a transcendence.

16. Luther, 76.
17. *Freedom*, 62.
18. *Freedom*, 62.
19. *Freedom*, 97.

Chapter 16

Modern Conceptions of Justice

"Temporal" Justice in Schopenhauer's Thought

Schopenhauer's conception of what might be called "temporal" justice (to distinguish it from his doctrine of eternal justice) is consistent with all the basic themes of his philosophy. "Temporal" justice is the type of justice that inhabits the world of phenomena, the world conditioned by time and space, the *principium individuationis*, and the *affirmation* of the will to live, where the "will" is constantly "sinking its teeth into its own flesh" as it were. Schopenhauer put it this way:

> The State is set up on the correct assumption that pure morality, i.e., right conduct from moral grounds, is not to be expected; otherwise it [i.e., the state] itself would be superfluous. Thus the State, aiming at well-being, is by no means directed against egoism, but only against the injurious consequences of egoism arising out of the plurality of egoistic individuals, reciprocally affecting them, and disturbing their well-being.[1]

1. *WWR*-1, 345.

The civic republicans and communitarians of our day, and of Thomas Jefferson's as well, tend to believe that the human being is perfectible, that civic virtue can be inculcated into him. Hence they tend to hold that one of the functions of the state, perhaps the main one in many of their minds, is to edify or educate the populace in civic virtue.[2] They tend to believe that "lawmaking is a process of *value creation* that should be informed by theories of justice and fairness."[3] One of the results of that mode of thought, that is, that human nature *is* perfectible and that the state *should* participate in the effort of perfectibility, has been the emergence of "political correctness" movements, whether of the political *right*, as in the days of Senator Joseph McCarthy, or of the political *left*, as in our own day, with agenda-driven groups seizing the reins of society and imposing their own brand of "right-think" on the populace at large.

With his very strong acceptance of the concept of the Calvinist-type understanding of original sin (as resulting in the "total depravity," that is, the *non*perfectibility, of human nature, except by a transcendent religious conversion), Schopenhauer, perhaps to his credit, would have none of the thinking of the civic republicans. Human nature is, according to Schopenhauer, very definitely *not* perfectible, except at the seldom-reached transcendent level of the denial of the will to live. Hence. Schopenhauer, in his theory of "temporal" justice, tended towards behaviorist principles. The state's only concern is the correction of conduct, not motives or minds:

> [W]ill and disposition, merely as such, do not concern the state at all; the *deed* alone does so (whether it be merely attempted or

---

2. See, e.g., Joseph Singer, "The Player & the Cards: Nihilism & Legal Theory," *Yale Law Journal* 94 (1984): 1.
3. William V. Eskridge, Philip P. Frickey, and Elizabeth Garrett, *Cases and Materials on Statutes and the Creation of Public Policy* (St. Paul, Minn.: West, 2001), 598 (emphasis added).

carried out), on account of its correlative, namely the *suffering* of the other party. Thus for the State the deed, the occurrence, is the only real thing; the disposition, the intention, is investigated only in so far as from it the significance of the deed becomes known.[4]

One might conclude from this that Schopenhauer's understanding of the role of the state, considered in relation to the individual, is of the distinctly libertarian stripe—only enough government to keep us from each other's throats.[5] At bottom, Schopenhauer's theory of "temporal" justice must be thought of as rather conventional. It is rights based, premised on the right not to have someone else's affirmation of his will to live encroach deleteriously on one's own life or property.

The more interesting conception of justice in Schopenhauer's writings is his doctrine of eternal justice. Schopenhauer's conception of eternal justice is anything but conventional. Recall that Schopenhauer regarded justice not as an epistemological construct, or even primarily as a virtue, but rather as a facet of *being* itself. Schopenhauer's doctrine is unique in that sense. That is not to say, however, that others whose views of "justice" ("eternal" or otherwise) are more conventional have not, in their mental meanderings, taken a Schopenhauerian turn or two.

A Personal Encounter with the Basics

From heaven's height
a heaven-born sympathy we drew.

---

4. *WWR*-1, 344.
5. For an excellent account of Schopenhauer's doctrine of temporal justice, see John E. Atwell, *Schopenhauer: The Human Character* (Philadelphia: Temple University Press, 1990), 193–201.

> To us the Maker gave a soul
> that mutual kindly feeling might us prompt
> to seek and render aid,
> and peoples form from scattered dwellers.[6]

Those words of Juvenal were on my mind as I sat down to participate in a teaching seminar comprising a dozen or so professors of Constitutional Law.[7] The topic of the seminar session was, and still is, a hotly debated issue in political and academic arenas: "The Philosophical Underpinnings of Constitutional Interpretation."

The seminar began, and we found ourselves searching for ways of identifying the philosophical underpinnings of those fundamental rights which, by a process of what law professors used to call "noninterpretive review,"[8] might exist in the shadowy, inexplicit, unexpressed parts of the Constitution.[9] Basic understandings of the concept of *justice* naturally suggested themselves to us, and we found ourselves exploring the various definitions of "justice" espoused by various legal philosophers.

As we progressed, our inquiry came quite close to the deepest level of moral thinking. We were unhampered by legalisms or even by direct constitutional restrictions. Our questions became something like this: What is the prime characteristic that ought to be present in human social interaction? Of course, we assumed "justice" to

---

6. Juvenal, *Satires*, XV, lines 146–53.
7. This section is excerpted from Raymond B. Marcin, "Justice and Love," *Catholic University Law Review* 33 (1984): 363.
8. See, e.g., John Hart Ely, *Constitutional Interpretivism*.
9. To some people, the argument that there can be inexplicit and even unexpressed "constitutional" rights seems to violate the very concept of a Constitution, the purpose of which would seem to be to make fundamental rights explicit and clearly expressed. Some might also suggest that the *judicial* creation of extra-constitutional rights, or rights outside "around the edges" of the constitutional text, circumvents and therefore violates the amendatory process within the Constitution itself.

be the broad answer and our immediate problem to be honing the concept down to its essence. And as we discussed the various offerings of various legal philosophers on the meaning of "justice,"[10] a common thread seemed to be discernible. They all seemed to be based on theories of *rights and entitlements,* or on how to organize a political system in which the rights and entitlements of human beings would be most fully recognized. "Justice," in other words, seemed to be grounded in an axiom that what ought to characterize human social interaction is a recognition of *rights and entitlements* — rights to acquire, to keep, to use, to own, to be let alone, to be helped. And this focus on rights and entitlements seemed, in turn, to be grounded in one human characteristic — the human wish or need to acquire, to keep, and to hold against other humans, in other words, acquisitiveness.

The words of Juvenal came to mind, and suddenly the thought struck. When we define "justice" in terms of human acquisitiveness and entitlements — more precisely, when we define "justice" *exclusively* in those terms — we may be creating a milieu for human social interaction which urges, perhaps determines, us to think in that context of acquisitiveness, possibly at the expense of other, more deeply human, qualities.

We were forced back into our original nonlegal, basically philosophical question of what is the prime characteristic that ought to be present in human social interaction. And this time a different, more startling answer suggested itself. And yet maybe it ought not to have been startling. If one resists the temptation to give an immediate answer to that question of what is the prime characteristic which ought

---

10. The seminal and somewhat question-begging definition of "justice" is that of Ulpian: *"Honeste vivere, alterium non laedere, suum cuique tribuere"* (Live honestly, cheat no one, and give each his due). Thomas Cooper, *The Institutes of Justinian,* § III (Philadelphia: P. Byrne, 1812), 6 (hereinafter, Cooper).

to be present in human social interaction, if one lets one's simplest and perhaps deepest feelings roll and jostle around a bit, the answer that percolates to the surface ignites one with the force of an ideal: *Love* ought to be present in human social interaction.

Perhaps, however, that thought is not such a great insight. Perhaps it is only a great insight for a *lawyer*. Schopenhauer, although he did not use the word "love" in the context of his treatment of justice, certainly had that insight in his radical doctrine of eternal justice. And perhaps the legal philosophers actually do begin their thought with that forceful ideal. But reality necessarily intrudes. It is precisely because human social interaction is not always characterized by love[11] that social rules must come into being—that we are forced to turn our attention to what Schopenhauer has referred to as "temporal justice." We simply cannot pause at that ideal of "love" and build a society around it, because love is not amenable to being organized, and is certainly not amenable to being compelled. Love, however, does seem to be something that is present in the collective

---

11. "Love" is, of course, a complex topic, not free of ambiguity and anomaly. Rollo May has identified four usages of the term: "There are four kinds of love in Western tradition. One is sex, or what we call lust, libido. The second is eros, the drive of love to procreate or create—the urge, as the Greeks put it, toward higher forms of being and relationship. A third is philia, or friendship, brotherly love. The fourth is devoted to the welfare of the other, the prototype of which is the love of God for man. . . . Every human experience of authentic love is a blending, in varying proportions, of these four." Rollo May, *Love and Will* (New York: Norton, 1969), 37. Irving Singer, on the other hand, has said that "concepts of eros and agape are ultimately inconsistent with one another. . . . Eros recognizes value and loves it—Agape loves, and creates value in its object." Irving Singer, *The Nature of Love* (Chicago: University of Chicago Press, 1966), 322. Erich Fromm has described "love" in a way that is probably most consistent with Schopenhauerian theory: "The basis for our need to love lies in the experience of separateness and the resulting need to overcome the anxiety of separateness by the experience of union." Erich Fromm, *The Art of Loving* (1956) (New York: Harper & Row, Perennial Library, 1974), 53. In Schopenhauer's thought, the "experience of separateness" is what exists at the level of phenomena, and the "experience of union," although difficult for the human being and only vaguely sensed at the level of phenomena, is a *reality* at the deep down, noumenal level.

psyche of human beings—the "heaven-born sympathy" and "mutual kindly feeling" of which Juvenal wrote—to be given, not wrested or demanded. Indeed, love wrested or demanded, most would agree, is no longer love. And so the legal philosophers have dismissed love as an organizing principle. We build our political systems on "temporal" *justice* rather than on love and, one has to admit (as does Schopenhauer), necessarily so, because the law must deal with what Schopenhauer called "temporal justice."

Still, however, no matter how sensitive and humane our definition of "justice" may be, we feel discomfort. In the microcosm of the individual human being, it is not unusual for feelings of discomfort to arise when one realizes, sometime during the maturing process, that one must temper the pure idealism of youth with the realities that one must often choose the lesser of evils and that not everyone's ideas of righteousness, justice, goodness, and truth comport with one's own. But the discomfort abates in the mature individual who, while still accepting the ideals of youth, has come to recognize those ideals as guides rather than dogmas—guides which cannot always be literally adhered to, but which strengthen and inform one's approach to social and moral questions. Few there are who would argue that the ideals of youth, however naive they may be, ought to be crushed when adulthood arrives. It is not their destruction but their shaping that matures a mind.

If now we turn our telescope around and look at the macrocosm of society, we can see the reason for our discomfort with the legal philosophers' definitions of justice. We have, somewhere deep in our collective psyche, the youthful ideal of *love*. But we have matured. We have come to recognize that the realities of the human situation—human imperfection, ideological pluralism—prevent us from building and nurturing a political system directly and solely on that youthful ideal. And so we build and nurture our political systems on concepts of *justice*. And perhaps the source of our continuing discomfort is the suspicion that in basing our concepts of justice on the wish or need to acquire, to keep, and to hold against others, regardless of how humanely or progressively we have treated it, we may be crushing rather than shaping that ideal of love. Schopenhauer would point to the fact of a deep down "felt consciousness" of the oneness that exists at the noumenal level of true reality.

The Problem with Conventional Concepts of "Justice"

Alf Ross, the Scandinavian author and apologist for the logical positivist school of jurisprudence, once analyzed the concept of "justice" as understood by the major legal philosophers and jurisprudential movements in political philosophy and was able to discern what have appeared to be the major components of the concept.[12] Beyond the somewhat question-begging Roman concept of giving everyone his due,[13] Ross noted the uniform occurrence of an *equality*[14] notion in the more content-oriented definitions of the term, a requirement in general that no one be arbitrarily subjected to treatment that differs from that accorded to any other person.[15] He further observed that since none of the definitions demanded absolutely equal treatment for individuals, there was a *rationality* component in the concept as well, a demand that differing treatment be in some way reasonable, a yardstick of evaluation for departures from absolute equality.[16] And in these features of content-oriented approaches to

---

12. Alf Ross, *On Law and Justice* (Berkeley: University of California Press, 1959) (hereinafter, Ross).
13. *"Honeste vivere, alterium non laedere, suum cuique tribuere"* (Live honestly, cheat no one, and give each his due). Cooper, 6.
14. The underpinning for an *equality* notion in Schopenhauerian theory, of course, would be his philosophy's recognition of a true inter*identity* among human beings at the deep down noumenal level of reality.
15. Ross, 269.
16. Ross, 270. In Schopenhauer's thought, because of its recognition of an

defining justice—the lack of a demand for absolute equality and instead a demand for some form of rationality governing departures from equality—Ross found the gremlin that untracks all such approaches, namely, ideological pluralism.

Ross may have overstated the case a bit (but maybe not) when he said: "All wars have been fought by all parties in the name of justice, and the same is true of the political conflict between social classes."[17] But there does seem to be just enough empirical truth in the assertion to give one pause. And it may not be, as Ross contended it was, "possible to advance every kind of material postulate in the name of justice,"[18] but Ross's main lesson is not lost on us. People may honestly, honorably, and rationally disagree about the meaning of the term "justice," and any approach to defining the term that does not take that fact into account is doomed. Ross's unsettling conclusion:

> To invoke justice is the same thing as banging on the table: an emotional expression which turns one's demand into an absolute postulate. . . . It is impossible to have a rational discussion with a man who mobilizes "justice," because he says nothing that can be argued for or against. His words are persuasion, not argument. The ideology of justice leads to implacability and conflict, since on the one hand it incites to the belief that one's demand is not merely the expression of a certain interest in conflict with opposing interests, but that it possesses a higher, absolute validity; and on the other hand it precludes all rational argument and discussion of a settlement.[19]

---

underlying interidentity among all human beings, departures from absolute equality justified on the ground of "rationality" would seem to bear a very high burden of persuasion.

17. Ross, 269.   18. Ross, 275.
19. Ross, 274–75.

Thus we see in Ross's critique of the justice definers an added reason for our feeling of discomfort. Not only does the *content* of most of the definitions bespeak acquisitiveness, the wish or felt need to acquire, to keep, and to hold against other human beings, but the very fact of *believing in* one's definition of justice leads to implacability and conflict. Our philosophers and theorizers are taking us far indeed from that youthful ideal.

The implications of all this for lawyers and all other participants and practitioners in a system of justice—particularly an Anglo-American system of justice—are obvious and ominous. Our legal systems are, predictably and predominantly, win-or-lose apparatuses. With acquisitiveness at the base of an ideal the very adherence to which perpetuates implacability and conflict, and with a group of professionals sworn to uphold that ideal, namely, lawyers, it seems foreordained that implacability and conflict will permeate the system. The purpose of lawyers seems to be to "win" for their client. The scholars among lawyers might, perhaps, view their purpose as lawyers as somewhat more complex than that (one would like to think); but in the end they even dally with the notion that their purpose is to win for their client *right-or-wrong*.[20] The arguments and tactics lawyers devise bespeak division and hostility. They are all too often, and sometimes all too close to irretrievably, figurative soldiers. They "war." Deep down, no one really feels good about this. Schopenhauer would suggest that deep down, we do not feel good about all this implacability and conflict because deep down we have this vague understanding at the noumenal level of true reality that we all share not only humanness, but also oneness, true identity—we are sinking our teeth into our own flesh. Lawyer and opposing counsel, client and opponent, even oppressor and oppressed, share humanness and

20. See, e.g., Monroe Freedman, *Lawyers' Ethics in an Adversary System* (Indianapolis: Bobbs-Merrill, 1975).

indeed identity itself at that noumenal level. And we all have a "felt consciousness," deep down, that what is needed in the area of human-social-interaction-gone-awry is not victory, but healing.

One wonders whether healing is or can be consistent with a concept of justice. The answer is not easy. Jean Anouilh included in his play "Becket" a brief colloquy on the meaning of justice. Moments before Becket was to be murdered in the Cathedral at Canterbury, he and Brother John, the somewhat feisty and very human monk who served him as acolyte, discussed a premonition of the attack:

> MONK . . . will it be today?
>
> BECKET. (Gravely) I think so, my son. Are you afraid?
>
> MONK. Oh, no. Not if we have time to fight. All I want is the chance to strike a few blows first; so I shan't have done nothing but receive them all my life. If I can kill one Norman first—just one, I don't want much—one for one, that will seem fair and right enough to me.
>
> BECKET. (With a kindly smile) Are you so very set on killing one?
>
> MONK. One for one. After that I don't much care if I am just a grain of sand in the machine. Because I know that by putting more and more grains of sand in the machine, one day it will come grinding to a stop.
>
> BECKET. (Gently) and on that day, what then?
>
> MONK. We'll set a fine, new, well-oiled machine in the place of the old one and this time we'll put the Normans into it instead. He asks quite without irony: That's what justice means, isn't it?
>
> BECKET smiles and does not answer him.[21]

---

21. Jean Anouilh, *Becket or The Honor of God* (New York: Signet Book, 1964), 125 (hereinafter, Anouilh).

It is a measure of our discomfort that Becket merely smiled, and did not answer Brother John. We might have expected Becket, who at that point in the play had developed into a wise and saintly man, to have answered Brother John with some saintly wisdom: "No, Brother John. Justice does not mean that. Justice means healing, and reconciling, and showing mercy even though the Normans have shown none." But Becket only smiled. Alf Ross was correct. The discomforting truth is that "justice" does indeed mean what Brother John thought it meant. It is indeed "just" that a wrongdoer be punished. And that being so, striking back at the oppressor was Brother John's entitlement and the oppressor's due. Hidden in Becket's smile is perhaps the image of Normans oppressing Saxons, then Saxons oppressing Normans, then Normans oppressing Saxons, et cetera ad nauseam—all in the name of "justice." One wishes that there were more to justice than the scale.

Occasionally we see, around the edges of the legal system, some reasons for optimism. One reason for optimism comes from the writings of Thomas Shaffer, who has analyzed the techniques of advocacy used by lawyers and come up with a revisionist definition, not of "justice," but rather of "advocacy"—a definition which nonetheless has a derivative impact on theoretical understandings of justice. "Advocacy," Shaffer insisted, "is largely, in fact, the practice of reconciliation."[22] Shaffer's model of lawyerly advocacy is the Prophet Nathan. Those of us schooled in Judeo-Christian traditions will recall that Nathan's difficult task was prosecutorial—to bring King David to justice. David had treated Uriah unjustly. Coveting and then taking Uriah's wife, Bathsheba, King David then sent Uriah to the war front and predictable death. Nathan successfully indicted David by telling him a similar tale of injustice, eliciting the king's own statement con-

---

22. Thomas Shaffer, *On Being a Christian and a Lawyer* (Provo, Utah: Brigham Young University Press, 1981), 111 (hereinafter, Shaffer).

demning the injustice, and then revealing to the king the analogy between the tale of injustice and the king's own treatment of Uriah.[23] Shaffer's point is that lawyers, as advocates, succeed most readily and most fully when they "as Nathan did, first engage conscience."[24] Shaffer does not mention Schopenhauer, but one thinks, as does Shaffer, of Mohandas K. Gandhi and Martin Luther King, Jr., who, as advocates, did indeed "first engage conscience" and achieved society-altering success.

However rare it may be in our system of justice, Shaffer's is a *healing* model of advocacy. Examples of that model occasionally surface in our system of justice. But it cannot be said to be the predominant model, or even the norm. The predominant model resides ensconced in, as Shaffer has indicated, our "professional tradition nourished by images of the champion." One must admit that it is not an unattractive norm, this image of a champion of another's cause, doing battle righteously, uncompromisingly—the knight in the right, the avenging angel bringing evil to its just reward. We like this norm, this image of the champion. It exudes to us courage, steadfastness in the face of danger, and many of the qualities that we feel ennoble us. And yet, while we readily hold to this image as, perhaps, the highest tradition of the bar, we once again feel discomfort.

A great value of Shaffer's work is that it helps pinpoint the source of the discomfort that we have with rights-based understandings of "justice." In a sense, the prophet Nathan was vindicating David's deprivation of Uriah's right to life, and in that sense Nathan's brand of "justice" was rights based. When we look closely at the Nathan example, however, we see a small, but significant distinction between the usual rights-vindication scenario and what Nathan did. Nathan was indeed a champion doing battle, but he was *not* an avenging an-

23. See 2 Samuel 12:1–7.
24. Shaffer, 116.

gel. Nathan's battle was not *against* David, but *with* him, champion and adversary alike joined in battle against the real enemy—injustice. In Nathan, we see all the virtues that we admire in the champion—undeniable courage, steadfastness in the face of danger—but we do not feel discomfort. The result of Nathan's advocacy was a healing. The result of an avenging angel's advocacy is—what? Vengeance? The evildoer getting his due? Frustration of the evildoer's mischievous design? The defeat, the come-uppance of the evildoer? We go on and on and we never come to a result that will completely satisfy us. The wrong is frustrated, but not righted. Injustice is excised, but justice not established. There is no *healing*.

But Nathan healed. And he did so by going through the process of engaging David's conscience, that is, by taking David out of the mental position that he (David) was in, the "veil of *Maya*" with all its well-insulated and guarded emotional predeterminates, and by placing him in a different mental position, an artificial position unclouded by the factors which had so hampered David's judgment in the Uriah incident. This "artificial-position" or process-based technique that resulted in the healing, in a reestablishment of justice, is curious. Nathan, in achieving not simply a just result, but justice itself, never defined justice. David became a just man once again, and "just" not simply on his own subjective level clouded and insulated by the ego defense mechanisms characteristic of the veil of *Maya*, but "just" on some objective level, really "just," healed—and all without an explanation of what justice objectively means.

One wonders whether Alf Ross would have as much, or indeed any, trouble with the notion of justice in the Nathan story. Nathan's is not the objective syllogistic advocacy model of "justice" (the rights-based model) that Ross so devastatingly defrocked,[25] that is, the "jus-

---

25. Ross.

tice is what I claim it to be, your conduct does not comport with that, therefore you have committed an injustice" model. Nathan's justice, strangely devoid of specific content, somehow leaves us convinced that there is content, content beyond mere self interest, important content, in the term, and a content that goes beyond rights and entitlements and acquisitiveness to something deeper, nobler—content that perhaps touches and builds upon the noumenal level of true reality. This artificial-position approach, lacking content yet seemingly bursting with meaning, merits further discussion.

Earlier, we saw, through the eyes of playwright Jean Anouilh, Thomas Becket's wan smile in the face of Brother John's fairness-and-equality type of definition of justice.[26] Brother John's definition of justice was, assuming that the Normans really were wrongdoers, conventional. We cannot help but believe that there is something unconventional about the Prophet Nathan's nondefinition of justice, a nondefinition that seems to have much more content, much more social worth, much more of a connection with true reality at the noumenal level—more of a connection with Schopenhauer's "eternal justice," than Brother John's. Those of us who like to categorize and classify will have no trouble with that seeming anomaly. As with "love," we use the term "justice" to cover more than one idea. In "justice" there are two concepts, the legal standard and the moral virtue. The categorizers among us, particularly those who adhere to legal positivism,[27] will have no trouble decreeing that the legal-standard notion of justice belongs to the discipline of law or jurisprudence, while the moral-virtue notion of justice belongs to the discipline of ethics or moral philosophy. Law regulates the external relations of human beings, whereas morality governs their internal life.

26. Anouilh, 125.
27. See, e.g., Edgar Bodenheimer, *Jurisprudence* (New York: McGraw-Hill, 1974), 73.

There is an attraction to this line of thought. At the level of phenomena, that is, the world around us, the legal standard of justice ought to rule. At the deep level of noumenal reality, the moral virtue of justice ought to rule. One might find the reasoning of this line of thought more persuasive, however, if the end result of Brother John's approach to justice (the legal-standard, rights-based type of justice), that is, the killing of Saxons by Normans and Normans by Saxons et cetera ad nauseam, were not so socially and politically *destructive*, and the end result of the Prophet Nathan's approach to justice (the moral-virtue, process-based type of justice), that is, the healing of King David, were not so socially and politically *constructive*. It may be that by categorizing and classifying and then filing "justice" so completely and with such exclusivity into two separate academic disciplines, we have overdone it a bit. Perhaps we ought to explore the thesis that the moral virtue of justice ought to inform the legal standard of justice to a far greater degree than it presently does. Perhaps we should look for something in the overall concept of "justice"—the ingredient that rendered the Prophet Nathan's non-definition of justice so full of meaning—and perhaps we should try to eliminate from our concept of "justice" whatever it is that has rendered Brother John's definition of justice so disturbing.

We are, however, left with a quandary at this point. If content-based definitions of justice tend to focus on entitlement and acquisitiveness and if the very idea of insisting upon a specific content for the concept of justice leads to implacability and conflict, then how are we to view this highest of our social ideals? Are we to eschew it in favor of another ideal, for example, the possibly higher ideal of love? But we have already granted that love is inappropriate as an organizing principle for a political society. If defining justice leads us nowhere, we may try the Prophet Nathan's idea of not defining justice. We might explore the "artificial position" approach.

"Artificial Position" Process-Based Conceptions of "Justice"

Perhaps the prophet Nathan's artificial-position approach struck us as novel. But in truth it is based on a sensibility that is at least as old as the teachings of Jesus, Hillel, Confucius, and Moses: The Golden Rule.[28] "Do unto others as you would have them do unto you" is so commonly known an artificial-position approach to the moral virtue of justice that we perhaps seldom plumb its true depth and certainly seldom if ever explore its relevance to systems of justice. Indeed Matthew quoted Jesus as saying that the Golden Rule sums up the law and the prophets.[29] But Jesus has not been the only one to mention the Golden Rule in the same breath with "law." The famed Categorical Imperative of Immanuel Kant is a version of the Golden Rule that is still having its impact on legal and moral theory: "There is . . . only one categorical imperative. It is: Act only according to the maxim by which you can at the same time will that it should become a universal law."[30]

Both the Golden Rule and Kant's Categorical Imperative are content-avoiding approaches to the meaning of justice. They prescribe no specific content at all and yet, as with Nathan's approach, they seem to be bursting with meaning and importance. They seem to draw upon a base of community or union among all human beings — perhaps a step towards a recognition of the oneness of all existence. It must be admitted, however, that Schopenhauer roundly critiqued Kant's Categorical Imperative,[31] but mainly on the basis that Kant focused it in a morality of *duty,* whereas Schopenhauer's morality was anything but a morality of duty. It was a morality of *virtue* or *character.* Be that as it may, these Golden-Rule-type approaches to moral

28. See, e.g., Matthew 7:12, Luke 6:31.
29. Matthew 7:12.
30. Kant, *Foundations*, 39.
31. *WWR*-1, 523.

quandaries use the *process* of placing the decision maker, the justice seeker, in an *artificial position,* that of committing one's act on oneself or on all of humankind. We often regard the Golden Rule and the more contemporary versions of the Categorical Imperative as platitudes, little axioms of experience that seem to work. We seldom ask why—what it is about human nature, humanness itself, that seems to give them validity and effectiveness. Perhaps it is the fault of the maxims themselves. They are process-oriented rather than content-based. And we tend to measure the truth of processes in terms of effectiveness, whereas we tend to measure the truth of content in terms of reasoning and grounding. But to ignore the reasoning and grounding of these process-oriented, artificial-position approaches to the meaning of justice is to ignore an opportunity to learn more about humanness. Again, it must be admitted that Schopenhauer would not likely agree with a process-oriented approach to moral problems, because "process" orientations usually entail a quest to assign meaning to a *duty*, and Schopenhauer's theory of morality was not duty based.

One finds it difficult to write of justice in the contemporary era without filtering it through the thought of John Rawls. Rawls's *A Theory of Justice*[32] puts forth a fully developed process-based, artificial-position approach joining Kantian moral theory to the political and contractarian ideas of Rousseau and Locke. Rawls sets forth a method of discovering (and justifying if you will) a society's fundamental principles of justice. His method involved the assumption of an artificial position, what Rawls called the *original position,* a situation in which rational, self-interested persons who have general knowledge about society and who appreciate the worth of moral principles, but who know nothing else about themselves—not their

32. Rawls, John, *A Theory of Justice* (Cambridge: Harvard University Press, 1971) (hereinafter, Rawls).

social status, their race, their preferences as to life style, not even their own sex—choose the general principles of justice for their society. Rawls's idea, of course, was to abstract from all those factors that make for bias or error in moral thinking. People under this *veil of ignorance,* as he called the original-position condition, can be trusted to come up with those general principles of justice which best comport with fairness.

The genius of Rawls's theory is that it accommodates the two ideals which most if not all content-based theories of justice strive to serve: individual liberty and social equality. The justice seekers in Rawls's original position are motivated by self-interest (the individual-liberty factor) and are deprived of knowledge of those factors that so often in the past have resulted in social inequality. Rawls's mechanism for deciding, the process, is fair; hence he has called his theory "Justice as Fairness."[33]

It is significant, and in some minds unfortunate, that Rawls posited that his justice seekers in the original position be *self*-interested. He was quite definite on this point, and expressly rejected "benevolence" as an original-position trait.[34] But curiously, almost paradoxically, Rawls insisted that a sense of justice is "continuous with" the love of humankind. How Rawls reconciled his requirement of a rational "self"-interest in his original-position theory with an outward-looking love of humankind can best be understood by first taking a slight detour into history.

The French Revolution is perhaps most commonly remembered today for its excesses. We find it difficult, recalling those excesses, to regard the French Revolution as a phenomenon of constructive political theory, and yet it was. A new social order was created—a new one—not the old vertical, hierarchical order, but a level, horizontal

33. Rawls, 11.
34. Rawls, 191.

order based on the two great needs of the day: freedom and equality. And again, focusing on those later excesses, it is difficult to credit the revolutionary theorists with genius. But they did possess genius, and perhaps it was best exemplified in their recognition that there is a root tension between the concepts of freedom and equality. Individual freedom results in social inequality, and imposed social equality curtails individual freedom. The solution of the revolutionary theorists was, of course, proudly proclaimed in the slogan of the French Revolution: Liberty, Equality, and Fraternity. The two conflicting political principles were seen as reconcilable, but only in the resolving agent of "fraternity."[35]

That the "fraternity" seized upon by the revolutionaries themselves ultimately proved to be the Freudian Oedipal brotherhood of destructive violence instead of some more benign manifestation is not, one may believe, the fault of the idea. Other conceptions of fraternity are possible. In fact, two millennia before the French Revolution, Aristotle saw the need for political fraternity, though not as a reconciling agent between liberty and equality.[36] In Aristotle's scheme of things, political fraternity was a benign force, empirically necessary in order to hold a society together and forestall revolution, but also somehow preexisting the political society; it was a force like Juvenal's "mutual kindly feeling," making political society a natural and necessary human enterprise. The origin of this benign force harks forward to Schopenhauer. According to Aristotle, the origin of

---

35. Today, under the intimidations of the "political correctness" movement, one might be tempted to try to avoid the single-sex connotation inherent in the word "fraternity" by using a gender-neutral synonym, e.g., "solidarity," "friendship," "unity," but both the slogan and Rawls used "fraternity," and I stay, for the most part, with that term.

36. Aristotle saw the need for political fraternity as a mediating link between the spheres of household, where in his Greek society slaves and women lacked individual liberty, and civic life. See Kronman, "Aristotle's Idea of Political Fraternity," *American Journal of Jurisprudence* 24 (1979):114, 115.

political fraternity is a kind of *interidentity* among human beings, recognition of the fact that humanness is shared and that other human beings are other "selves."[37]

John Rawls certainly understood the significance of fraternity in connection with freedom and equality, and his understanding of that significance occupies a focal point in his theory of justice. Rawls's "veil of ignorance" placed the justice seeker in a most awkward position. Rawls required that the person in the "original position" discharge his or her task on the basis of self-interest, but he left precious little of the "self" to be interested in. There seems to be no way of knowing which general principles of justice are especially in one's own self-interest if one is in Rawls's original position. And that seems to be the point of it all. Thus positioned, one may be expected to cultivate and assert one's own advancement and advantage, but never at the cost of making another person less advantaged, because one never knows but that one might actually be that other person. This led Rawls to his "difference principle": the person in the original position, under the veil of ignorance, would not want to have greater advantages unless the situation would also be to the benefit, in some degree at least, of others who are less well off. The difference principle seems to be what keeps Rawls's theory of justice relentlessly progressive. And it is this difference principle that Rawls identified with the term "fraternity."[38] It *is* fraternity in Rawls's scheme of things. In truth, Rawls's self-interest-based idea of fraternity does seem to be much of an improvement on the esprit-de-corps kind of fraternity, based on "us-again-them" sentiments, which found shuddering ex-

---

37. See Kronman,"Aristotle's Idea of Political Fraternity," *American Journal of Jurisprudence* 24 (1979):114, 126–27. It pains us today that Aristotle either did not see or did not feel the need of pursuing this interidentity concept in the context of the existence of slavery in his society. His approach seems to have been to analyze humanness, individuality, selfness and the like, and in the political context to apply that analysis to "households" rather than to individuals.

38. See Rawls, 106.

pression in the later excesses of the French Revolution (and, one might project, in Brother John's idea of justice). It is quite clearly rights-based, that is, based on that quality of acquisitiveness, the human wish or need to acquire, to keep, and to hold against other humans, albeit with an edge of tolerance.

There is, however, that other interpretation of "fraternity," the one that seemed to underlie Aristotle's approach to the idea, and Rawls was sensitive to it, while dismissing it. It is the kind of fraternity based on benevolence or altruism. Why did Rawls require one in the original position to act out of self-interest, instead of out of other-interest, altruism? The answer to this question brings us to the crux of what is paradoxically both the connection and the distinction between justice and love in Rawls's theory.

One is tempted to suggest that it matters little if at all whether the person in the original position under the veil of ignorance is self-interested or is other-interested, simply because he or she has no way of knowing which general principle of justice will benefit the self more than the other. One has no way of knowing whether one is a giver or a taker. If one wishes to be a giver, one is still led inexorably to Rawls's difference principle—and perhaps the more so if one is truly an altruist. One would be forced by his or her own ideal of other-interest to tolerate some self-benefit, just as the self-interested person in the original position is forced to tolerate some other-benefit. In neither case is the person in the original position in any position to know who the self is and who the others are. And there is a tantalizing third type of interest besides self-interest and other-interest. There is what might be called *"all-interest,"* probably best encapsulated in the familiar scriptural injunction to love all others as one loves oneself.[39] An original-position person who has that third type of

39. Leviticus 19:18, 34; Matthew 19:19, 22:39; Mark 12:31, 33. The altruistic other-interest is, perhaps, best encapsulated in the familiar story of the Good Samaritan. Luke 10:29–37.

"*all*-interest" would also be accepting of the difference principle, but perhaps with a more leveling effect, since to the "all-interested" person both self- and other-interest must be served. An *all*-interest perspective would also—and almost by definition—be consistent with Schopenhauer's "felt consciousness" of the oneness of reality.

But Rawls would have none of this. He stayed with self-interest.[40] A sense of justice, within Rawls's original-position device, is linked to self-interest. The love of humankind, Rawls asserted, differs from the sense of justice, in that love of humankind prompts acts of supererogation, that is, acts above and beyond the call of duty. In the final analysis, Rawls's theory of justice, although showing promise, stays at the level of phenomena, and fails to ground itself in the interidentity that permeates the world at the deep down noumenal level.

Gandhi Revisited

That brings us back to the jurisprudence of Mohandas K. Gandhi. We do not often think of Gandhi as a lawyer, much less as a legal scholar, and yet he was both. Perhaps his stature as a modern-day saint gets in the way. Or perhaps we neglect his legal scholarship because we don't find in his writings analyses of Holmes, Pound, Austin, or Bentham. We cannot seem to take seriously as a legal

---

40. Professor Darwall has argued to the contrary and has seemed to see a form of other- or all-interest in Rawls's formulation of the difference principle. In Professor Darwall's view: "Because of the veil of ignorance the original position is not a perspective of self-interest, but rather of an interest in selves, or individuals as such. . . . What is crucial to the perspective is the idea of a concern for individual rational beings, or selves, as such." S. Darwall, "Is there a Kantian Foundation for Rawlsian Justice?," reprinted in *John Rawls's Theory of Social Justice: An Introduction*, ed. H. Gene Blocker and Elizabeth H. Smith (Athens, Ohio: Ohio University Press, 1980), 340, 341. Rawls himself has made statements which seem both to support and to contradict Professor Darwall's reading: "[T]he combination of mutual disinterest and the veil of ignorance achieves the same purpose as benevolence," and "[T]he persons in the original position are assumed to take no interest in one another's interests." Rawls, 148, 147, respectively.

scholar one who has not bowed in obeisance before those framers of the Western legal mind. What we find in Gandhi's legal scholarship is an eclectic and seemingly narrow sampling of the speeches of Jesus, the thought of Tolstoy, and the works of the nineteenth-century American transcendentalists. And what we *may* find in Gandhi's legal scholarship, if we look deep enough, is an understanding of "justice" that will comport with Schopenhauer's doctrine of eternal justice, that is, an understanding of "justice" that will be grounded in the deep down level of true, noumenal reality.

There is a reason for the seeming narrowness and selectivity of Gandhi's legal scholarship. In its *practical* applications, his thought was original. Gandhi applied his thought to social justice, to group politics. And the testing ground for the truth of Gandhi's views on justice and love was not logic or precedent, but (as Holmes would have appreciated) experience.

In the context of the above inquiry into the process-based concepts of justice, that is, the artificial-position context, what Gandhi did, paradoxically, was to bring things full circle. We began our inquiry by decrying the fact that most definitions of "justice" are rights based; they speak in terms of entitlement and serve the motivation of acquisitiveness. We then examined the process-based, "artificial-position" theories that seem to succeed in some measure, but never completely satisfactorily, in introducing motivations other than acquisitiveness and content other than entitlement into concepts of justice. Through an in-the-shoes-of-the-other-person device, they seemed to place the justice seeker in a mode of tolerance and acceptance.

The way in which Gandhi brought all of this full circle is that his concept of justice was not based on some self-aggrandizing right, but rather on an "other-focused" (and indeed an "*all*-focused") right — the right to have the oppressor *see* the justice or injustice of his or her activity by viewing its concrete results on his or her victim, and derivatively on all other human beings, including the oppressor. What Gandhi relied on for the effectiveness of this full-circle, rights-based, artificial-position approach was, of course, the fact that human beings see other human beings as other "selves," that is, that an identification takes place. It is a concept grounded in the identity, *not* of interests, but of *being,* among human beings—that ontological identity which gives rise to sensibilities of justice and of love alike. In other words, it is based on the identity of being that exists at the deep level of true, noumenal reality. Gandhi's concept of justice thus relies on the very underpinning of Schopenhauer's doctrine of eternal justice.

The particulars of Gandhi's views developed and changed over the years because they depended so much on events and experiences, and any thumbnail sketch of his "theory of justice" is bound to be suspect. But the following quotation from his explanation of the Hindu concept of *"ahimsa"* expresses the grounding of his concept of justice quite well:

> We punish thieves, because we think they harass us. They may leave us alone; but they will only transfer their attentions to another victim. This other victim however is also a human being, *ourselves in a different form,* and so we are caught in a vicious circle. The trouble from thieves continues to increase, as they think it is their business to steal. In the end we see that it is better to endure the thieves than to punish them. The forebearance may even bring them to their senses. By enduring them we realize that thieves are *not different from ourselves,* they are our brethren, our friends, and may not be punished. But whilst we may bear with the thieves, we may not endure the affliction. That would only induce cowardice. So we realize a further duty. Since we regard the thieves as our kith and kin, they must be made to realize the kinship. And so we must take pains to devise

ways and means of winning them over. This is the path of ahimsa.[41]

Under Gandhi's "ahimsa" one does not stop at nonresistance. One must take steps to apprise the evildoer affirmatively of his or her human identity, indeed his or her human *inter*identity. Gandhi's "ahimsa" has been referred to not as an ethic of *non*resistance to evil, but rather as an ethic of *nonviolent* (Gandhi himself disliked the adjective "passive")[42] *resistance* to evil. The name one gives to the ethic, however, seems far less important than its paradoxical message: Evil is most effectively resisted through nonresistance. Gandhi's discovery was that by accepting the physical consequences of the unjust act, but also (and this most importantly) by bringing the fact of that injustice and the fact of *shared human identity* to the attention of the evildoer, that is, by "first engaging conscience,"[43] one was bringing about a situation of true, thorough, and ultimate justice instead of the forced physical representation of justice with which courts and lawmakers must content themselves.

There is an obvious attraction in Gandhi's theory of justice/love. Almost by definition and certainly by design, if it works, it solves the problem of recidivism. But criticisms abound. One criticism is that Gandhi's theory works outside, against, or perhaps "on" the government's institutions and organs of justice, and not "with," or as a part of, them. Another criticism is that Gandhi's theory is "other-worldly," unrealistic, too ideal. To give Gandhi his due, however, his nonviolent-resistance doctrine is seldom delved into deeply by academicians, and the common belief that it amounts to sketchy idealism is

---

41. Mohandas K. Gandhi, *Nonviolent Resistance (Satyagraha)* (New York: Shocken Books, 1951), 41 (emphasis added) (hereinafter, Gandhi, *Nonviolent*).

42. Gandhi, *Nonviolent*, 375. See also Mohandas K. Gandhi, *All Men Are Brothers: Autobiographical Reflections*, ed. Krishna Kripalani (New York: Continuum, 1958), 91, 92.

43. Shaffer, 116.

unwarranted. Gandhi placed great stress on method and effectiveness. This is apparent in Gandhi's oft-misunderstood teaching on fasting as a method of nonviolent resistance:

> Fasting in Satyagraha[44] has well defined limits. You cannot fast against a tyrant, for it will be a species of violence done to him. You invite penalty from him for disobedience of his orders but you cannot inflict on yourselves penalties when he refuses to punish and renders it impossible for you to disobey his orders so as to compel infliction of penalty. Fasting can only be resorted to against a lover, not to extort rights but to reform him, as when a son fasts for a father who drinks.[45]

Gandhi's life-long arena was not speculative philosophy, but rather social justice. He sought the justice that was missing in the British colonial rule over India, in the Hindu treatment of the untouchables,[46] in the relationships between Hindu and Moslem Indians,[47] in the apartheid of South Africa. And his method of achieving justice was, quite simply, love. Not love, the sentiment, the appetite, but love, the activity, the work. And not just any well-intentioned activity or work suffices in Gandhi's system. "That action alone is just," Gandhi once wrote, "which does not harm either party to a dispute."[48] In Gandhi, we see the melding of justice and love, the appropriate relationship between the two. In Gandhi's example, we may also find a theory of justice that is consistent with Schopenhauer's doctrine of eternal justice.[49]

44. Literally, "Truth-force": the name Gandhi gave to his theory/movement.
45. Letter to Mr. George Joseph, reprinted in Gandhi, *Nonviolent*, 182.
46. Gandhi, *Nonviolent*, 180.
47. In which endeavor, he did use the fasting technique. See Letter to Mr. George Joseph, reprinted in Gandhi, *Nonviolent*, 182.
48. Mohandas K. Gandhi, *Collected Works*, 233; also quoted in Erik Erikson, *Gandhi's Truth* (New York: W. W. Norton, 1969), 342.
49. *WWR*-1, 351.

Chapter 17

Schopenhauer and Contemporary Political Thought

The implications of Schopenhauer's theory of eternal justice for contemporary political and jurisprudential thought are as sweeping as they are profound. Contemporary political and jurisprudential thought, plagued as it is by polar inconsistencies in its views of humanness itself, and without a metaphysical grounding for its tenets and propositions, has been drifting back toward early-twentieth-century forms of philosophical pragmatism.[1]

On the one hand, legal economists and public-choice theorists

---

1. See, e.g., Steven J. Burton, *An Introduction to Law and Legal Reasoning*, 2nd ed. (Boston: Little, Brown, 1995); Stephen M. McJohn, "On Uberty: Legal Reasoning by Analogy and Peirce's Theory of Abduction," *Willamette Law Review* 29 (1993): 191; Daniel C. K. Chow, "A Pragmatic Model of Law," *Washington Law Review* 67 (1992): 755; Dennis M. Patterson, "Law's Pragmatism: Law as Practice and Narrative," *Virginia Law Review* 76 (1990): 937; "Symposium on the Renaissance of Pragmatism in American Legal Thought," *S. California Law Review* 63 (1990): 1753 ; and Steven D. Smith, 'The Pursuit of Pragmatism," *Yale Law Journal* 100 (1990): 409.

sometimes see the human being as nothing more or less than "an egoistic, rational, utility maximizer."[2] On the other hand, contemporary civic republicans and other communitarians see the human being as an entity fully capable of an altruistic cooperative solidarity.[3] Both views cannot be true, yet both views command responsible adherents, leading some, like John Rawls and Adam Smith long before him, to strive for a melding of the two seemingly inconsistent views,[4] with problematic success in each case.

Schopenhauer's theory of justice at large, along with his theory of eternal justice in particular, accommodates both views of humankind with ease. At the phenomenal level, the level at which we live our daily lives, the human being *is* an egoistic, rational utility maximizer, wallowing in the chaos of self-interest which permeates the affirmation of the will to live. And yet, according to Schopenhauer, that level of phenomenal reality is but an illusion. Deep down at the unfathomable level of the noumenal, the human being is different. At the noumenal level, the human being *is* a oneness, a unity that goes even beyond comm-unity, beyond social siblinghood, a unity of all encompassing identity, an identity at the level of being itself.

The legal economists and public-choice theorists sense the phe-

2. Dennis C. Mueller, *Public Choice II* (Cambridge: Cambridge University Press, 1989).

3. See, e.g., Michael Sandel, *Liberalism and the Limits of Justice* (Cambridge: Cambridge University Press, 1982); Kathleen M. Sullivan, "The Republican Civic Tradition: Rainbow Republicanism," *Yale Law Journal* 97 (1988): 1713; and Robert Cover, "Nomos and Narrative," *Harvard Law Review* 97 (1983): 4.

4. Rawls's "veil of ignorance" device can be seen as a melding of the two views of humankind, starting as it does from a premise of self-interest but yielding communitarian results. See Raymond B. Marcin, "Justice and Love," *Catholic University Law Review* 33 (1984): 363, 372–78. Adam Smith's device for melding the two views was the "invisible hand" whereby somehow the result of individuals acting in their own self-interests is social betterment. See Adam Smith, *An Inquiry Into the Nature and Causes of the Wealth of Nations*, vol. 1, bk. 4, chap. 2 (1776), 9 (Indianapolis: Liberty Classics ed., Oxford University Press, 1976), 456; and *The Theory of Moral Sentiments*, Part IV, chap. 1 (1759), 10 (Indianapolis: Liberty Classics ed., Oxford University Press, 1976), 184–85.

nomenal level of everyday reality. The civic republicans and other communitarians sense the noumenal level of eternal reality. Each grasps reality at a level which is incomplete, and contemporary jurisprudence has come to sense that fact, that is, that neither the communitarians nor the economists have successfully taken the measure of humankind. Hence the attraction of philosophical pragmatism with its skeptical attitude towards truth, wherein "the ideas of truth and falsehood, in their full development, appertain exclusively to the experiential method of setting opinion."[5]

Contemporary quantum physicists, as we have seen, tell us that there are two levels of reality, or two "worlds" inhabited by us—a Newtonian world at the level of perception in which we are ruled by the principle of cause and effect, discreteness, and the arrow of time—and a quantum world at the unobservable level of bare existence in which all is one and one is all and one and all are driven by the angst of tendency and probability. Schopenhauer, as we have seen, tells us the very same thing in the context of justice. We inhabit two worlds—a legal world at the level of perception in which we rule and are ruled by responsibilities and duties, rights and entitlements, all controlling for what would otherwise be the law of the jungle—and a noumenal world at the unfathomable level of true reality in which the law of the jungle can only be understood as an inexorable demand of eternal justice, angst feeding on itself.

Schopenhauer's dualism yields some interesting conclusions for contemporary jurisprudential theorists. At the phenomenal level, the level of everyday life, Schopenhauer is one with the libertarians, legal economists, and public choice theorists. Jurisprudence should be behaviorist.[6] Schopenhauer, who denied the freedom of the will at

---

5. Justus Buchler, ed., *Philosophical Writings of Peirce* (New York: Dover Publications, 1955), 37.

6. See Posner, 169–96. Posner has concluded that "[b]ehaviorism is the only practical working assumption for law, and its dangers have been exaggerated." Posner, 178.

the phenomenal level, could only see the law in behaviorist terms. He found the essence of the behaviorist credo in Seneca's *Laws:* "No sensible person punishes because a wrong has been done, but in order that a wrong may not be done."[7] Law must operate at the phenomenal, not the noumenal, level, and at that phenomenal level, self-interest reigns supreme. An other-interest (i.e., a mandate that everybody be altruistic) cannot be legislated. The only thing that can be legislated is a course of conduct whose results would be the same as those that would ensue if people *were* other-interested. The law can only affect behavior, and cannot effect a change in will and disposition: "[W]ill and disposition, merely as such, do not concern the State at all; the *deed* alone does so (whether it be merely attempted or carried out), on account of its correlative, namely the *suffering* of the other party. Thus for the State, the deed, the occurrence, is the only real thing. . . ."[8] Posner put it in more contemporary language: "The behaviorist approach seems to leave no room for appeals to conscience, for a sense of guilt, of remorse; it seems to strip the moral as well as the distinctively human content from the criminal law. The pragmatic reply is, So what?"[9]

Schopenhauer's lesson for the civic republicans and other communitarians of today is that what they seem to be trying to bring to the fore—a fundamental sense of solidarity among all human beings—is a chimera. In one sense it already exists, but at an all-but-unreachable level. Striving for it at the level of phenomena, where self interest reigns, only results in its eventual negation, well exemplified in the us-against-them attitude which reached shuddering excesses in the aftermath of the altruistically republican era of the French Revolution[10] and in countless other less dramatic political ad-

---

7. *WWR*-1, 349.   8. *WWR*-1, 344.
9. Posner, 177–78.
10. See Raymond B. Marcin, "Justice and Love," *Catholic University Law Review* 33 (1984): 363, 373.

ventures in altruistic solidarity,[11] including governmentally mandated "speech codes" and political-correctness impositions. In Zen, and perhaps in contemporary political terms, it is like trying to rid one's self of the right side of one's body by constantly moving more and more to the left.[12]

Schopenhauer's only answer to the duality was his advocacy of the transcendental and mystical denial of the will to live. He saw the denial of the will to live as the only way of reaching the otherwise unreachable and incorporating into one's consciousness that fundamental, noumenal truth about human existence—and that only on the level of the individual.

Earlier in this study it was suggested that the Schopenhauerian approach to justice might lead quite naturally in two directions: (1) the direction taken much earlier by Martin Luther, and (2) the direction taken somewhat later by Mohandas K. Gandhi. By far, the more interesting of the two directions jurisprudentially is the one taken by Gandhi. Schopenhauer himself, since he confined his discussion of the denial of the will to live to the possibility of its achievement in the life of the *individual,* would have (had he not been an atheist) felt quite comfortable with the Lutheran doctrine of individual salvation by rebirth in faith.

If the individual, according to both Schopenhauer and Luther (and many Christian and other theologians), can experience a true rebirth—a change of character from a world- and flesh-oriented "Adam" nature to a deeper spirit-oriented "Christ" nature, can socie-

11. See, e.g., Raymond B. Marcin, "Justice and Love," *Catholic University Law Review* 33 (1984): 363, passim.

12. Of course, one may apply the same thought to the legal economists and public-choice theorists, who in similar terms may be trying to rid themselves of, or at least ignore, the left sides of their bodies by constantly positioning themselves more and more towards the right. The thought here is that both perspectives are valid, but both are also limited. Needed, of course, is a transcendent perspective, which Schopenhauer would identify as the denial of the will to live.

ty-at-large undergo a similar experience? The lives and works of Gandhi and his followers, including Martin Luther King, Jr., are testament both to the possibility and to the difficulty of such a social metamorphosis.

It may be that the civic republicans and other communitarian theorists of today are trying, consciously or unconsciously, to do exactly that, that is, to touch the noumenal unity which lies at the deepest level of human existence, to free us from the individual self-interested utility maximization of the old "Adam" nature and bring us to the new spiritual *aion* of enlightenment of the "Christ" nature. The civic republicans and other communitarians *do* seem to want to lead us *from* a present age or *aion* characterized by something unpleasant—an unsatisfying centering on isolating and divisive individual and group self-interests—*to* a new salvational age or *aion* characterized by something that has been missing—a productive spirit of solidarity and a recognition of a unifying interidentity among all of humankind.

If so, Schopenhauer, for all his crusty misanthropy, may have something to contribute to their quest, for Schopenhauer's doctrine of the denial of the will to live is a look at salvation from the vantage point of the *un*saved. It is not the effort of a Gautama Siddhartha or a Mohammed or a Christian mystic to explain what he or she has seen on the other side of "enlightenment." It is the affirmation of someone who has *not been* there, that something *is* there, something ineffable, yet real—something worth the quest.

Bibliography

Books

Atwell, John E. *Schopenhauer: The Human Character*. Philadelphia: Temple University Press, 1990.

——. *Schopenhauer on the Character of the World: The Metaphysics of Will*. Berkeley: University of California Press, 1995.

Anouilh, Jean. *Becket or The Honor of God*. New York: Signet Book, 1964.

Aquinas, Saint Thomas. *Summa Theologiae*. In five volumes. Trans. Fathers of the English Dominican Province under the title *Summa Theologica*. Allen, Tex.: Christian Classics, 1981.

Bible. Douay-Rheims.

Blake, William. *The Portable Blake*. Ed. A. Kazin. Middlesex: Penguin Books, 1974.

Blocker, H. Gene, and Elizabeth H. Smith, eds. *John Rawls's Theory of Social Justice: An Introduction*. Athens, Ohio: Ohio University Press, 1980.

Bodenheimer, Edgar. *Jurisprudence*. New York: McGraw-Hill, 1974.

Bohm, David. *Wholeness and the Implicate Order*. London: Routledge, 1980.

Buchler, Justus, ed. *Philosophical Writings of Peirce*. New York: Dover Publications, 1955.

Burton, Steven J. *An Introduction to Law and Legal Reasoning*. 2nd ed. Boston: Little, Brown, 1995.

Burtt, E. A. *The Teachings of the Compassionate Buddha*. New York: Mentor Books, 1955.

Capra, Fritjof. *The Tao of Physics*. 25th Anniversary ed. Boston: Shambhala, 1999.

Cassina, Ubaldo. *Saggio Analitico Sulla Compassione*. Parma: Nella Stamperia Reale, 1772.

Collins, James. *A History of Modern European Philosophy*. Milwaukee: Bruce Publishing Company, 1954.

Collins, Larry, and Dominique LaPierre. *Freedom at Midnight*. New York: Avon, 1975.

Cooper, Thomas. *The Institutes of Justinian*. Philadelphia: P. Byrne, 1812.
Copleston, Frederick, S.J. *Arthur Schopenhauer: Philosopher of Pessimism*. Andover, Hants, U.K.: Burns, Oates & Washbourne, 1946.
Davies, Paul. *The Cosmic Blueprint: New Discoveries in Nature's Creative Ability to Order the Universe*. New York: Simon & Schuster, 1988.
———. *God and the New Physics*. New York: Simon & Schuster, 1983.
———. *The Mind of God: The Scientific Basis for a Rational World*. New York: Simon & Schuster, 1992.
Davies, Paul, and John Gribben. *The Matter Myth: Dramatic Discoveries That Challenge Our Understanding of Physical Reality*. New York: Simon & Schuster, 1992.
Davies, P. C. W., and J. R. Brown. *The Ghost in the Atom*. Cambridge: Cambridge University Press, 1986.
De Leonardis, David J. *Ethical Implications of Unity and the Divine in Nicholas of Cusa*. Washington, D.C.: The Council for Research in Values and Philosophy, 1998.
Dillard, Annie. *Teaching a Stone to Talk: Expeditions and Encounters*. New York: Harper, 1982.
Dionysius the Areopagite. *The Mystical Theology*. Internet at: "esoteric.msu.edu/VolumeII/MysticaslTheology.html". Also found in *Pseudo Dionysius: The Complete Works*. Trans. Colm Luibheid. Mahwah, N.J.: Paulist Press, 1987.
Einstein, Albert. *Ideas and Opinions*. New York: Crown Publishers, 1954.
———. *Relativity: The Special and the General Theory*. New York: Crown Publishers, 1961.
Erikson, Erik. *Gandhi's Truth*. New York: W. W. Norton, 1969.
Eskridge, William V., Philip P. Frickey, and Elizabeth Garrett. *Cases and Materials on Statutes and the Creation of Public Policy*. St. Paul, Minn.: West, 2001.
Fest, Joachim C. *Hitler*. Trans. Richard and Clara Winston. New York: Harcourt Brace Janovich, 1974.
Freedman, Monroe. *Lawyers' Ethics in an Adversary System*. Indianapolis: Bobbs-Merrill, 1975.
Fromm, Erich. *The Art of Loving* (1956). New York: Harper & Row, Perennial Library, 1974.
Gandhi, Mohandas K. *All Men Are Brothers: Autobiographical Reflections*. Ed. Krishna Kripalani. New York: Continuum, 1958.
———. *An Autobiography: The Story of My Experiments With Truth*. Trans. Mahadev Desai. First published in two volumes in 1927 and 1929 in the Gujarati language. Boston: Beacon Press, 1957.
———. *The Collected Works of Mahatma Gandhi*. In 100 volumes. New Delhi: Publications Division of the Government of India, 1958–94.
———. *Nonviolent Resistance Satyagraha*. New York: Shocken Books, 1951.
Glendon, Mary Ann. *Rights Talk: The Impoverishment of Political Discourse*. New York: Free Press, 1991.
Granfield, David, O.S.B. *Heightened Consciousness: The Mystical Difference*. New York: Paulist Press, 1991.

Greene, Brian. *The Elegant Universe: Superstrings, Hidden Dimensions, and the Quest for the Ultimate Theory.* New York: W. W. Norton, 1999.
Greene, Brian. *The Fabric of the Cosmos: Space, Time, and the Texture of Reality.* New York: Alfred A. Knopf, 2004.
Gribben, John. *In Search of Schrödinger's Cat: Quantum Physics and Reality.* New York: Bantam Books, 1984.
———. *Q is for Quantum: Particle Physics from A to Z.* London: Weidenfeld & Nicholson, 1998.
———. *Schrödinger's Kittens and the Search for Reality: Solving the Quantum Mysteries.* Boston: Little, Brown, 1995.
Hamlyn, David W. *Schopenhauer: The Arguments of the Philosophers.* London: Routledge, 1985.
Hardon, John, S.J. *The Catholic Catechism: A Contemporary Catechism of the Teachings of the Catholic Church.* Collegeville, Minn.: Liturgical Press, 1975.
Heisenberg, Werner. *Physics and Philosophy: The Revolution in Modern Science.* (1958). Amherst, N.Y.: Prometheus Books, 1999.
Herbert, Nick. *Quantum Reality: Beyond the New Physics.* Garden City, N.Y.: Anchor Books, 1987.
Hitler, Adolf. *Mein Kampf* (1927). Trans. Ralph Manheim. Boston: Houghton Mifflin, 1971.
Janaway, Christopher. *Schopenhauer.* Oxford: Oxford University Press, 1994.
Janaway, Christopher, ed. *The Cambridge Companion to Schopenhauer.* Cambridge: Cambridge University Press, 1999.
Jeans, Sir James. *Physics and Philosophy.* Cambridge: Cambridge University Press, 1943; New York: Dover Publications, 1981.
Jung, Carl G. *The Archetypes and the Collective Unconscious.* Trans. R. F. C. Hull. Princeton, N.J.: Princeton University Press, 1969.
———. *Memories, Dreams, Reflections.* Trans. R. and C. Winston. New York: Random House, 1963.
———. *Symbols of Transformation.* Trans. R. F. C. Hull. Princeton, N.J.: Princeton University Press, 1969.
Jung, Carl G., and Carl Kerenyi. *Essays on a Science of Mythology.* Trans. R. F. C. Hull. Princeton, N.J.: Princeton University Press, 1949.
Kaku, Michio, and Jennifer Thompson. *Beyond Einstein: The Cosmic Quest for the Theory of the Universe.* New York: Anchor Books, 1995.
Kaltenmark, Max. *Lao Tzu and Taoism.* Trans. Roger Greaves. Stanford, Calif.: Stanford University Press, 1965.
Kant, Immanuel. *Foundations of the Metaphysics of Morals* (1785). Trans. Lewis White Beck. Indianapolis: Bobbs-Merrill, 1959.
Kant, Immanuel. *The Critique of Pure Reason* (1781 and 1787). Trans. Norman Kemp Smith. New York: St. Martin's Press, 1965.
Knox, Ronald A. *Enthusiasm: A Chapter in the History of Religion.* First published by Oxford University Press, 1950. Notre Dame, Ind.: University of Notre Dame Press, 1994.
Malin, Shimon. *Nature Loves to Hide: Quantum Physics and the Nature of Reality; A Western Perspective.* New York: Oxford University Press, 2001.

Luther, Martin. *Commentary on the Epistle to the Romans* (1552). Trans. J. Mueller. Grand Rapids, Mich.: Zondervan, 1954.
———. *On the Bondage of the Will.* Ed. Schmidt. 1707.
Magee, Bryan. *The Philosophy of Schopenhauer.* Rev. ed. Oxford: Clarendon Press, 1997.
May, Rollo. *Love and Will.* New York: Norton, 1969.
May, William E. *An Introduction to Moral Theology.* Rev. ed. Huntington, Ind.: Our Sunday Visitor Publishing Division, 1994.
McGill, V. J. *Schopenhauer: Pessimist and Pagan.* New York: Brentano's, 1931.
Molinos, Miguel de. *The Spiritual Guide.* Trans. an anonymous Quietist. Written, 1678; printed at Venice, 1685; London: 1688.
Mueller, Dennis C. *Public Choice II.* Cambridge: Cambridge University Press, 1989.
Nadeau, Robert, and Menas Kafatos. *The Non-Local Universe: The New Physics and Matters of the Mind.* Oxford: Oxford University Press, 1999.
Nichol, Lee, ed. *The Essential David Bohm.* London: Routledge, 2003.
Nicholas of Cusa. *Nicholas of Cusa: Selected Spiritual Writings.* Trans. H. Lawrence Bond. New York: Paulist Press, 1997.
Pagels, Heinz R. *The Cosmic Code: Quantum Physics As the Language of Nature.* New York: Bantam Books, 1982.
Payne, Robert. *The Life and Death of Adolf Hitler.* New York: Praeger, 1973.
Planck, Max. *The Philosophy of Physics.* Trans. W. H. Johnston. New York: W. W. Norton, 1936.
Plato: Collected Dialogues. Ed. Edith Hamilton and Huntington Cairns. New York: Pantheon Books, 1961.
Pope Innocent XI. *Coelestis Pastor.* November 20, 1687. Internet at "ewtn.com/library/PAPALDOC/I11COEL.HTM".
Posner, Richard A. *The Problems of Jurisprudence.* Cambridge: Harvard University Press, 1990.
Powell, James N. *The Tao of Symbols.* New York: Quill, 1982.
Rawls, John. *A Theory of Justice.* Cambridge: Harvard University Press, 1971.
Ross, Alf. *On Law and Justice.* Berkeley: University of California Press, 1959.
Rousseau, Jean Jacques. *Emile.* Trans. Barbara Foxley. London: J. M. Dent, 1993.
Safranski, Rüdiger. *Schopenhauer and the Wild Years of Philosophy.* Trans. Ewald Osers. Cambridge: Harvard University Press, 1990.
Sandel, Michael. *Liberalism and the Limits of Justice.* Cambridge: Cambridge University Press, 1982.
Schopenhauer, Arthur. *Essays and Aphorisms.* Trans. R. J. Hollingdale. Middlesex: Penguin Books, 1970.
———. *On the Basis of Morality* (1841). Trans. E. F. J. Payne. Oxford: Berghahn Books, 1965; rev. ed. 1995.
———. *On the Freedom of the Will* (1841). Trans. Konstantin Kolenda. Indianapolis: Bobbs-Merrill, 1960.
———. *Parerga and Paralipomena* (1851). 2 vols. Trans. E. F. J. Payne. Oxford: Clarendon Press, 1974.

---. *The World as Will and Representation*, vol. 1 (1819). Trans. E. F. J. Payne. New York: Dover Books, 1969.

---. *The World as Will and Representation*, vol. 2 (1844). Trans. E. F. J. Payne. New York: Dover Books, 1969.

Schrödinger, Erwin. *My View of the World.* Originally published by Paul Zsolnay Verlag GMBH, 1961. Trans. Cecily Hastings. Woodbridge, Conn.: Ox Bow Press, 1983.

Shaffer, Thomas. *On Being a Christian and a Lawyer.* Provo, Utah: Brigham Young University Press, 1981.

Singer, Irving. *The Nature of Love.* Chicago: University of Chicago Press, 1966.

Smith, Adam. *An Inquiry Into the Nature and Causes of the Wealth of Nations* (1776). Indianapolis: Liberty Classics ed., Oxford University Press, 1976.

---. *The Theory of Moral Sentiments* (1759). Indianapolis: Liberty Classics ed., Oxford University Press, 1976.

Sunstein, Cass R. *After the Rights Revolution: Reconceiving the Regulatory State.* Cambridge: Harvard University Press, 1990.

Talbot, Michael. *The Holographic Universe.* New York: Harper Perennial, 1991.

Theologia Germanica. Trans. Susanna Winkworth. London: Macmillan, 1893. Also available in a rev. version: *Theologia Germanica.* Trans. Susanna Winkworth. Ed. Joseph Bernhart. New York: Pantheon, 1949. More easily available on the Internet at "www.passtheword.org/DIALOGS-FROM-THE-PAST/theogrm1.htm".

The Theologia Germanica of Martin Luther. Trans. Bengt Hoffman. Classics of Western Spirituality Mahwah, N.J.: Paulist Press, 1980.

Toland, John. *Adolf Hitler.* 2 vols. Garden City, N.Y.: Doubleday, 1976.

Watts, Alan. *The Supreme Identity: An Essay on Oriental Metaphysic and the Christian Religion.* New York: Vintage Books, 1972.

---. *The Two Hands of God: The Myths of Polarity.* New York: Collier Books, 1963.

---. *The Way of Zen.* New York: Pantheon, 1958.

Whitney, Charles A. *The Discovery of Our Galaxy.* New York: Alfred A. Knopf, 1971.

Wilber, Ken, ed. *Quantum Questions: Mystical Writings of the World's Greatest Physicists.* Boston: Shambhala, 2001.

Wolter, Alan B. *Duns Scotus on the Will and Morality.* Washington, D.C.: The Catholic University of America Press, 1986.

Zimmer, Heinrich. *Philosophies of India.* Ed. J. Campbell. Princeton, N.J.: Princeton University Press, 1951.

Zimmern, Helen. *Schopenhauer: His Life and Philosophy.* London: Longmans Green, 1876.

Zukav, Gary. *The Dancing Wu Li Masters: An Overview of the New Physics.* New York: Perennial Classics, 2001.

Articles

Chow, Daniel C. K. "A Pragmatic Model of Law." *Washington Law Review* 67 (1992): 755–825.
Cover, Robert. "Nomos and Narrative." *Harvard Law Review* 97 (1983): 4–68.
Chroust, Anton-Hermann. "The Fundamental Ideas in Saint Augustine's Philosophy of Law." *American Journal of Jurisprudence* 18 (1973): 57–79.
———. "Natural Law and 'According to Nature' in Ancient Philosophy." *American Journal of Jurisprudence* 23 (1978): 73–87.
———. "The Philosophy of Law of the Early Sophists." *American Journal of Jurisprudence* 20 (1975): 81–94.
———. "The Philosophy of St. Thomas Aquinas: His Fundamental Ideas and Some of His Historical Precursors." *American Journal of Jurisprudence* 19 (1974): 1–38.
Ely, John Hart. "Constitutional Interpretivism: Its Allure and Impossibility." *Indiana Law Journal* 53 (1978): 399–448.
Gardbaum, Stephen A. "Law, Politics, and the Claims of Community." *Michigan Law Review* 90 (1992): 685–760.
Kronman, Anthony. "Aristotle's Idea of Political Fraternity." *American Journal of Jurisprudence* 24 (1979): 114–38.
Levin, Avner. "Quantum Physics in Private Law." *Canadian Journal of Law and Jurisprudence* 14 (2001): 249–60.
Maguire, Joseph P. "Plato's Theory of Natural Law." *Yale Classical Studies* 10 (1947): 151–78.
Marcin, Raymond B. "Justice and Love." *Catholic University Law Review* 33 (1984): 363–91.
———. "Schopenhauer's Theory of Justice." *Catholic University Law Review* 43 (1994): 813–65.
McJohn, Stephen M. "On Uberty: Legal Reasoning by Analogy and Peirce's Theory of Abduction." *Willamette Law Review* 29 (1993): 191–235.
Patterson, Dennis M. "Law's Pragmatism: Law as Practice and Narrative." *Virginia Law Review* 76 (1990): 937–96.
Ratzinger, Joseph Cardinal. "Conscience and Truth." *Paper presented at the 10th workshop for bishops.* Dallas, Tex., February, 1991.
Singer, Joseph. "The Player & the Cards: Nihilism & Legal Theory." *Yale Law Journal* 94 (1984): 1–70.
Smith, Steven D. "The Pursuit of Pragmatism." *Yale Law Journal* 100 (1990): 409–49.
Sullivan, Kathleen M. "Rainbow Republicanism." *Yale Law Journal* 97 (1988): 1713–23.
"Symposium on the Renaissance of Pragmatism in American Legal Thought." *Southern California Law Review* 63 (1990): 1569–751.
Symposium. "The Republican Civic Tradition." *Yale Law Journal* 97 (1988): 1493–608.
Tribe, Laurence. "The Curvature of Constitutional Space: What Lawyers Can Learn from Modern Physics." *Harvard Law Review* 103 (1989): 1–39.

Van Sistine, Michael J., and Bruce Meredith. "The Legality of Early Retirement Incentive Plans: Can Quantum Physics Help Resolve the Current Uncertainty." *Marquette Law Review* 84 (2001): 587–657.

Wright, R. George. "Should the Law Reflect the World?: Lessons for Legal Theory from Quantum Mechanics." *Florida State University Law Review* 18 (1991): 855–82.

Index

Adam, 76, 87, 110–12, 130–31, 144; and Eve, 130–31; and Jesus, 110–12
affirmation of the will-to-live, 68, 70–73, 77, 79, 82, 93, 98, 101–3, 105–7, 109, 117, 124, 128, 131, 147, 175, 179
ahimsa, xvi, 97–98, 171–72
Allegory of the Cave, Plato's, 33–34
anamnesis, 85–86
Anesaki, 100
Anuilh, Jean, 157, 161, 181
Aquinas, Saint Thomas, 74–92, 181
archetypes, 36, 85, 109–10, 183
Aristotle, 166–68, 186
arrow of time, 176
artificial position, 160–71
Aspect, Alain, 50
Atwell, John E., 149, 181
Austin, John, 169

Becket, Saint Thomas, 157–58, 161, 181
Bell, John, 50
bellum omnia contra omnes, 70, 82, 102
Benedict XVI, Pope. *See* Pope Benedict XVI
Bentham, Jeremy, 169
Berkeley, George, 15, 23–24, 26–27
Blake, William, 53, 62, 181
Blocker, H. Gene, 169, 181
Bodenheimer, Edgar, 161, 181
Bohm, David, x, 52–57, 62–63, 181, 184

Bohr, Neils, 39–40
Brahman (Brahmanism), 58, 60, 99–100, 105, 110, 117, 124–26, 132
Brown, J. R., 41, 57, 182
Buchler, Justus, 176, 181
Buddha (Buddhism, Buddhist), xiv, 7, 100, 105–7, 110, 117, 124–26, 132
Burtt, E. A., 100, 181
Byron, Lord, 37

Cain, 75
Capra, Fritjof, 30, 44–45, 51, 53–54, 181
Cassina, Ubaldo, 138, 181
cat, Schopenhauer's, xi–xiii, 54, 111
cat, Schrödinger's, xii–xiii, 41–43, 49, 54, 111, 183
categorical imperative, 2, 115, 163–64
causality, principle of, 8, 14, 16, 21–26, 32, 46, 96, 143
Chow, Daniel C. K., 174, 186
Chroust, Anton-Hermann, 81, 91–92, 186
Chuang Tsu, 100
civic republicanism (civic republicans), xvi–xvii, 148, 175–77, 179, 186
collective unconscious, Jungian, 36, 109, 183
Collins, James, 15, 181
Collins, Larry, 97, 181
community (communitarians), xvi, 87, 148, 163, 175–76, 179, 186

compassion, 2–4, 95, 100, 114, 134, 137–38
complementarity, principle of, 39–40
Confucius, 163
conscience, 72–78, 84–88, 159–60, 172, 177, 186
consciousness, felt. *See* felt consciousness
contradiction, principle of, 85–86, 88
Cooper, Thomas, 151, 154, 182
Copenhagen interpretation, 40–43
"Copernican Revolution", Kant's, 11, 14–15, 21, 23–24, 40, 66
"Copernican Revolution", Schopenhauer's, 20
Copernicus, Nicholas, 11–14
Copleston, Frederick, S.J., 5, 9–10, 113, 125, 182
Council of Trent, 125
critical legal studies, xvi–xvii

Darwall, S., 169
Davies, Paul, 182
Davies, P. C. W., 41, 57, 182
De Leonardis, David J., 57, 182
denial of the will-to-live, 65, 69, 70–71, 79–80, 83, 104–13, 117–18, 120–22, 124–25, 132–33, 135, 146, 148, 178–79
Dillard, Annie, 20, 182
Dionysius the Areopagite, 121, 182
Donne, John, 53
Duns Scotus, 75, 185

Eckhart, Meister, 119–21
egoism, 68, 70, 82, 102, 135–37, 147
Einstein, Albert, xiii–xiv, xvii, 31, 39, 48–50, 54, 61, 182, 183
Einstein-Podolsky-Rosen (EPR experiment), 49–50, 55
Ely, John, 150, 186
EPR experiment. *See* Einstein-Podolsky-Rosen
Eskridge, William V., 148, 182
eternal justice, 67, 83, 93–103, 112, 147, 149, 161, 171, 173–76
eternal law, 83–84, 88, 91
evil, 75, 86, 88, 93–96, 101, 130–31, 135, 146, 153, 159, 172

Fall of Adam, 76, 87, 110, 112, 130–31
felt consciousness, 73, 77–78, 154, 157, 169
Fénelon, Francois, 117, 119, 121
Fest, Joachim, 3, 95, 182
Fichte, Johann, 1–2, 25–26
fish (David Bohm's fish illustration), 54–56
Francis of Assisi, Saint, 138
Freedman, Monroe, 156, 182
freedom of the will, 4, 108, 135, 139, 140–46, 176, 184
French Revolution, 165–66, 168, 177
Frickey, Phillip P., 148, 182
Fromm, Erich, 152, 182

Gandhi, Mohandas K. (Mahatma), xvi, 65, 95–101, 112, 138, 159, 169–73, 178–79, 182
Gardbaum, Stephen A., xvi, 186
Garden of Eden, 130, 132
Garrett, Elizabeth, 148, 182
Glendon, Mary Ann, xvi, 182
God, 28, 48, 58, 76, 78, 81–84, 87–91, 94, 111, 118, 121–23, 127–35, 144–45, 152, 157, 181–82, 185
"god" ("gods"), 82, 94, 129
good, 75–79, 84, 86–90, 94, 120, 127, 130–31, 134–35, 145, 153
Goethe, 7, 59
Golden Rule, the, 163–64
Granfield, David, O.S.B., 132–33, 182
Gribben, John, xii–xiii, 13, 40–43, 49, 182–83
Guyon, Madame, 119

Hamlyn, David W., 33, 141, 183
Hardon, John, S.J., 112, 183
Hegel, xvi, 1–2, 8, 15–17, 19, 26
Heisenberg, Werner, 12–13, 39–40, 46, 183
Herbert, Nick, 46–49, 183
Hillel, 163
himsa, 96–98
Hitler, Adolf, 3, 95, 182–85
Hobbes, Thomas, 70, 73, 102
hologram, 56

Idea (Platonic). *See* Platonic Ideas (Forms)
idealism, 15, 23–24, 26, 60, 153, 172

implicate order, 52-53, 56, 62-63, 181
individuation, 19, 29, 51-52, 63-67, 96, 98, 105, 110, 113, 147
Innocent XI, Pope. *See* Pope Innocent XI

Janaway, Christopher, 10, 113, 183
Jerome, Saint, 75
John Paul II, Pope. *See* Pope John Paul II
Jung, Carl, 36, 65, 109-10, 183
justice, xi, xv-xvii, 11, 62, 65, 67, 69, 80, 83, 91, 93, 95, 97-100, 112, 137, 140, 147-78, 181, 184, 186
Juvenal, 150-51, 153, 166

Kafatos, Menas, 50, 184
Kaltenmark, Max, 100-101, 183
Kantian flaw, the, 23-26, 136
Kant, Immanuel, xiv, xvi, 1-2, 7, 11-18, 20-21, 23-27, 30-32, 40, 52, 60, 66, 72, 114-15, 131, 134, 136, 163-64, 169, 183
Kerenyi, Carl, 110, 183
King, Jr., Rev. Dr. Martin Luther, 159, 179
Knox, Msgr. Ronald A., 119, 129-30, 183
Kripalani, Krishna, 172, 182
Kronman, Anthony 166-67, 186

LaPierre, Dominique, 97, 181
law. *See* eternal law
law-and-economics movement, xvi-xvii, 174-76, 178
law of the jungle, 64, 93, 102, 176
Laws of Manu, 72
Lee, Mother Ann, 119
Levin, Avner, xv, 186
Locke, John, 8, 27, 164
love, xv-xvi, 9, 36, 65, 120, 123, 127-28, 139, 150, 152-54, 161-62, 165, 168-73, 175, 177-78, 184-86
Luther, Martin, 109, 121-23, 127-28, 134-35, 144-46, 178-79, 184-85

Magee, Bryan, xiv, 5-10, 21, 31, 77, 79, 95, 108-9, 142, 184
Maguire, Joseph P., 81, 186
Majer, Friedrich, 7
malice, 137

Marcin, Raymond B., xv-xvi, 65, 150, 175, 177-78, 186
matter, xiv, 27-32, 39, 44, 46-48, 51-52, 182
May, Rollo, 152, 184
May, William E., 87-88, 90, 184
Maya, 105-6, 113, 160
McGill, V. J., 5, 184
McJohn, Stephen M., 174, 186
Meredith, Bruce, xv, 187
metaphysics, xv-xvii, 1, 8, 11-16, 21, 23, 28, 39, 53, 58-59, 61, 69, 73, 76, 93, 96, 99, 109, 111, 113-15, 135-38, 140, 144, 174, 181, 183, 185
Molinos, Miguel de, 118-20, 129, 184
Moses, 111, 163
Mother Teresa, 158
Mueller, Dennis C., 175, 184

Nadeau, Robert, 50, 184
Nathan, Prophet, 158-63
natural law, xvi, 74-92, 186
neoplatonism, 117
new legal process jurisprudence, xvi
Nirvana, 105, 107, 123, 125-26, 152
noumenal level, 26, 46, 69, 72, 152, 154, 156-57, 161-62, 169-71, 175-79

O'Connor, Justice Sandra Day, 81-82, 86-87
ontological oneness, 2, 59-60
ontology (ontological), xv-xvii, 2, 11, 32-33, 35, 40, 44, 48, 59-60, 76, 80, 96-97, 137-38, 171
Original Sin, 76-77, 80, 87, 91, 105-6, 112, 124, 129, 148
Oxenford, John, 10

Pagels, Heinz, 38-40, 184
particle, 13, 39-41, 46-49, 51, 53, 55, 183
Patterson, Dennis M., 174, 186
Payne, E. F. J., xi, 2, 4, 8, 184-85
Payne, Robert, 3, 95, 184
Planck, Max, 38-39, 53, 184
Plato, 14, 33-36, 81, 85, 142, 184
Platonic Ideas (Forms), 8, 14, 33-37, 85-86, 95, 114, 139-42
Platonism, 7, 83

plurality, 29, 48, 51–52, 60, 63–67, 69, 101–2, 104, 107, 110, 113–14, 136, 147
Podolsky, Boris, 48–50
Pope Benedict XVI, 86. *See also* Ratzinger, Joseph Cardinal
Pope Innocent XI, 118–19, 129, 184
Pope John Paul II, 86
Posner, Richard A., xvi, 176–77, 184
Powell, James N., 110, 184
principium individuationis, 29, 51, 62, 65–66, 98, 147
problem of evil, the, 93–96, 101, 130–31, 135, 146
Pseudo-Dionysius. *See* Dionysius the Areopagite

quantum theory, xi–xv, xvii, 10, 12–13, 21, 30, 32, 39–40, 44–63, 99, 111, 176, 185–87
Quietism, xvii, 57, 116–33, 184

Ratzinger, Joseph Cardinal, 86, 186. *See also* Pope Benedict XVI
Rawls, John, xvi, 164–69, 175, 181, 184
relativity, theory of, xiv, 31, 39, 48, 50, 182
representation (re-presentation), xi–xii, 7–8, 19, 21, 24, 26, 32–33, 56, 64, 69, 72, 101, 119, 135, 140, 172, 185
right and wrong, 69–72
Rosen, Nathan, 48–50
Ross, Alf, 154–56, 158, 160, 184
Rousseau, Jean Jacques, 114, 164, 184

Safranski, Rüdiger, 4–5, 9, 24–25, 184
Sandel, Michael, 175, 184
Satan, 129
Satyagraha, xvi, 172–73, 182
Schelling, Friedrich, 1–2, 26
Schopenhauer, Arthur, *passim*; Aquinas and, 74–79; departure from Kant, 18–27; Kant's influence on, 11–17; Gandhi and, 95–101, 169–73; Goethe's influence on, 7; life of, 1–10; Luther and, 109, 134–38, 144–46, 178; Majer's influence on, 7. *See also* affirmation of the will-to-live; cat, Schopenhauer's; compassion; "Copernican Revolution", Schopenhauer's; denial of the will-to-live; egoism; eternal justice; freedom of the will; individuation; Platonic Ideas; plurality; problem of evil; quantum theory; Quietism; representation (re-presentation); right and wrong; temporal justice; thing-in-itself; will; will to live
Schrödinger, Erwin, xii–xiii, xvii, 9–10, 41–43, 49, 52, 54, 58–62, 99–100, 111–12, 183, 185
Shaffer, Thomas, 158–59, 172, 185
Shakers, 119
Singer, Irving, 152, 185
Singer, Joseph, 148, 186
Smith, Adam, 175, 185
Smith, Elizabeth H., 169, 181
Smith, Steven D., 174, 186
space, xv, 2, 8, 11, 12–16, 18–22, 29–30, 32–34, 35–36, 39–40, 44, 46, 48, 50–53, 55, 57, 61–63, 65–67, 83, 96, 99, 101, 104, 110, 113, 115, 126, 131, 135, 142–44, 147, 176, 183
space-time, 131
Spinoza, Benedict de, 20
Suarez, Francisco, 20
suicide, 5, 106, 108
Sullivan, Kathleen M., 175, 186
summum bonum, 78–79
Sunstein, Cass R., xvi, 185
synderesis, 74–75, 77–78, 84–88, 90–91

Talbot, Michael, 56, 185
Tat tvam asi, 60, 99
Tauler, Johannes, 119, 121
temporal justice, 147–49
Theologia Germanica, 117, 119, 121–23, 127–28, 185
thing-in-itself, 13, 19, 21–23, 25–26, 28–29, 32, 34–35. 46, 51, 62, 66, 69, 96, 98, 101–2, 104, 106–9, 115, 128, 136, 141–43
time, xiii, 2, 8, 11–16, 18–19, 21–22, 29–30, 32, 34–36, 39–40, 44, 46, 48, 50–53, 57, 61–63, 65–68, 83, 96, 99, 101, 104, 110, 113, 115, 126, 131, 135, 142–44, 147, 176, 183
Toland, John, 3, 95, 185

Tolstoy, Leo, 80, 95, 158, 170
transcendental aesthetic, Kant's, 2, 14, 20–21
transcendental logic, Kant's, 14, 21
Tribe, Laurence, xv, 186

Ulpian, 151
uncertainty principle, Heisenberg's, 12–13, 39, 48

Van Sistine, Michael J., xv, 207
Vedanta, 2, 29, 59–60
veil of ignorance, Rawls's, 167–69, 175
veil of *Maya*. *See Maya*

Watts, Alan, 28, 185
Whitney, Charles A., 14, 185
will, xi–xii, 2, 4, 7–10, 18–23, 28–32, 34–37, 45–48, 51–52, 55–58, 62–66, 68–73, 75–80, 82–83, 85–87, 89, 93, 96, 98, 101–2, 104–10, 114–33, 135–36, 139–49, 152, 163, 175–79, 181, 184–85
will-to-live, 63–65, 68–69, 72, 77, 79–80, 82–83, 93, 98, 101, 104–6, 108–10, 117–18, 120–22, 125, 127, 129–33, 135–36, 144, 146–49, 175, 178–79. *See also* affirmation of the will-to-live; denial of the will-to-live
Wolter, Alan B., 75, 185
Wright, R. George, xv, 187

Zimmer, Heinrich, 106, 185
Zimmern, Helen, 5, 185
Zukav, Gary, 53, 185

In Search of Schopenhauer's Cat: Arthur Schopenhauer's Quantum-Mystical Theory of Justice was designed and composed in Walbaum by Kachergis Book Design of Pittsboro, North Carolina. It was printed on 60-pound Natures Natural and bound by Thomson-Shore, Inc., of Dexter, Michigan.

www.ingramcontent.com/pod-product-compliance
Lightning Source LLC
Chambersburg PA
CBHW032035290426
44110CB00012B/814